MW01620482

The
Nature of Beauty

The Nature of Beauty

The Nature of Beauty

Text by

Martha and Jay Shuler

Photographs by

Jay Shuler

Edited by

William P. Baldwin

Patty B. Fulcher and V. Elizabeth Turk

Published by:
The Village Museum
McClellanville, S.C.

Text Copyright 2003 Martha M. Shuler and William P. Baldwin
Photograph copyright 2003 Martha M. Shuler
All Rights Reserved

No part of this book may be reproduced or transmitted in any form or by any means, electronic or mechanical, including photocopying and recording, or by any information storage or retrieval system, without permission in writing from the publisher.

First Edition

ISBN 0-9740091-0-5

Published by
The Village Museum
PO Box 595
McClellanville, SC 29458

This book was made possible in part by grants from an anonymous donor and The Village Museum.

All royalties from the First Edition of this book will support The Village Museum.

Printed by Bang Press
Brainerd, Minnesota

ACKNOWLEDGEMENTS

Special thanks to Gary Bronson of McClellanville Computers. His interest and time made this book possible.

Thanks to:

Selden B. Hill, Director, The Village Museum

Sam Savage, Wizard

Dawn Ohman of Bang Press

Rebecca Blanton, Emmy Bronson, Betsy and George Geer,
Sara Harken, Alice Jordan, Phyllis McGrew, John McWilliams,
Sonny Morrison, Buzzy Porter, Candice Reeves, Graham and Judy Solomons,

Jim and Ali

Lil, Aaron, and Malcolm

And to all our other friends who have given their patient encouragement.

The Nature of Beauty

In Memory of Jay

And for all my beloved family and friends
who make it possible for me to continue
to live at my paradise called Doe Hall.

M.M.S

The Nature of Beauty

INTRODUCTION

Photographer Ansel Adams once defined art as "the giving and taking of beauty." It's a Zen notion, this apparent negation, this simultaneous act of both giving and taking. In short, the act of creation requires more than an ordinary taking and giving. In short, the act of truly "looking" can't be put into words. As Adams explained, the artist is quite literally baring his soul.

Art is both the giving and taking of beauty. I suspect Jay Shuler considered art in that way as well, for like Ansel Adams, what Jay photographed was by the very process of elimination a portrait of himself. Not an actual portrait, of course, for Jay's subject was nature. Jay's subject was the untrampled world that he worked so diligently to protect. His subject was America's wilderness. From Maine's parks to Mexico's jungles, from the Dakota Badlands to the Everglades—together Jay and his wife Martha criss-crossed our continent, camping, birding, enjoying each other's company and photographing. This is their story.

At 6'3" Jay Shuler was a gentle giant—a man large in both size and spirit. He was always ready with a kind and encouraging word. He was always ready to teach, always ready to learn. Jay was a generous and giving friend and we who were his friends often took his talent and intelligence for granted. But then Jay was not one to draw attention to himself. Starting in the early 1950's, he'd made a living as a nature photographer which in South Carolina at that time was unheard of. Jay had found a niche, though, providing slides for schoolroom nature studies and he continued to do this for almost

20 years. Then with a subsequent career in the U. S. Park Service he continued to photograph. In addition, he wrote newspaper columns, poetry, hundreds of articles and filmstrips and even a full-length biography—all connected in one way on another with natural history. When he retired from the Park Service, just the listing of his work ran to 28 pages, and for the purposes of this book, we've drawn a bit from all of it.

In a very real sense, though, this is Martha Shuler's book for her reminiscences give it structure. And the reader should be warned that despite the apparent randomness of her memory, there is a structure to this account, one that relies most often not on a chronological progression but an emotional one. What follows is about love and joy and also about loss, and even the seemingly off-handed comments carry a message. Martha and Jay were the sort of couple who are always mentioned in unison. You didn't go to see Martha. You didn't go to see Jay. You went out to Martha and Jay's. They were far more than husband and wife—but you're about to learn that for yourself.

Patty Fulcher and I had known them well for twenty-five years or more and in 1999 we approached the now widowed Martha about doing an oral history of her life and of her and Jay's life together. We'd just completed a similar project with South Carolinian Genevieve Peterkin which was published as *Heaven is a Beautiful Place*, and we saw in Martha another excellent storyteller—insightful, warm and humorous. I suspect, in part, it was to humor us that Martha agreed, and off and on for over a year, she spoke her tales into the tape recorder.

Packed in the attic were the newspaper columns and on my bookshelf at home were Jay's poetry and prose. Our book grew and we realized with a heart-rending certainty that Martha and Jay's story was an exceptional one. The photographs came at the end, an incredible bonus that was also packed away in the attic. Worked up as slides, Jay had seldom printed these, and even for those who knew of them, their intense beauty as prints came as a surprise—especially since many were the so called "rejects" from his numerous projects. With over 5000 to choose from, Atlanta photographer Elizabeth Turk took over the process of editing these. Breaking the light-box into preferential columns of A, B, and C, she patiently winnowed away for weeks and came up with most of the handful included here.

By modern standards Jay's camera equipment was incredibly simple. A 35mm Nikon and two or three lenses are all he carried, but through that viewfinder he saw with the eye of an artist. These photographs are not only beautiful, they speak of beauty for they reflect that inner process by which the artist gives voice to the perceptions of joy and pain that are entailed. Jay's writings, especially the poetry, often did the same.

What is art? We hope this book is an example. Reader, we hope you find in these pages both the giving and taking of beauty. We hope you find a new way of seeing.

This is a love story.

This is the story of Martha and Jay.

William P. Baldwin
February 2003

Chapter One

Our Early Years

MARTHA: South Carolina

I met Jay in October of 1933. I was just two weeks old. By the time I was born Daddy had given up farming and had moved his family into the little village of McClellanville. Jay lived two doors down. Jay was three. Mama was changing my diaper and Jay's mother sat him down on the bed beside me and said, "Now, Mary, they're compromised. They'll have to get married." So there was nothing else to do if he was a true gentleman.

Oh, Jay and I were great friends. At the age of 12 he just seemed to grow and grow. He was all bony arms and legs. I'll never forget Jay racing across a field and accidentally stepping on a baby rabbit. When he saw he'd killed it, he sat down and cried. I knew then what a wonderful person he was. I loved him like a brother. He would go in the woods studying nature. He went all the time and I just had to go along. He said, "All right, you can follow me around but you've got to get over your own fences." And I did. Years later when we were engaged, he turned around and held out his hand for me to jump over a fallen tree. I knew then that he loved me. Such a romance!

But that was later. We weren't childhood sweethearts. We didn't go together in high school except for one dance. Cilla had the mumps so I filled in for her. Jay asked, "Do you think you could get together a dress in time to go to the dance with me because Cilla's got the mumps?" I said, "Sure, I'll go." I had a wonderful time but didn't dance even once with Jay. I recall that my principal partner that night held one foot steady and then moved the other foot, then dragged the steady foot around and around in circles.

Jay never did like to dance. After we were engaged he invited me upstate to Clemson College for a big Harry James dance weekend. I packed a long dress and went. We were walking along the river and I said shouldn't we get back and dress for the dance. He said we weren't going. I said, "Didn't you ask me over for the dance?" He said, "No." He said, "No, but if you want to hear the music we can go and walk around outside the hall." We skipped that event. But on special occasions Jay would dance with me.

Now, back to when I was 12. Cilla's daddy taught her to drive. Cilla was my friend so she taught me. Anytime our car was in the yard, we'd jump in and I'd drive around the circle. This was in 1939 and Daddy probably had a Ford, but he liked Chrysler products and ended up with Chryslers. He ended up with a Cordova which he gave me just before he died.

Anyway, one Saturday, Daddy said, "Child, you can drive, can't you?"

I said, "Oh, yes."

He said, "Well, I want you and Em to go and get your mother."

I said, "You mean Grahamville?" Grahamville was almost to Savannah, Georgia. At least 130 miles away.

He said, "Yes."

So my sister Emily and I got in the car and took off from McClellanville. I was 12. Emily was 8 1\2. We traveled 40 miles of narrow concrete road, most of which was through the country, and then started up the even narrower Cooper River bridge. Two big camel humps that allowed ocean-going ships to pass under. Waves breaking about a mile below and in the other lane cars and trucks coming almost at you. I was halfway across and looked over at Emily. She wasn't in the passenger's seat. Somehow she'd gotten under the dashboard. But I was having the time of my life. Being twelve years old and out on my own for the first time.

I'm surprised we even knew the way. I had to drive through Charleston and even after that I was faced with all sorts of turn offs. But I had traveled that road many times. We spent every summer in Grahamville, a village much like our own. I'm not sure how our grandmother and aunt put up with us, but we'd stay all summer and play with our Horry cousins.

Well, we showed up in Grahamville and Mama came out to greet us.

She said, "Where is your father?"

We said, "Daddy sent us for you." Of course, Mother was furious, and she insisted on doing all the driving on the way back.

But I was proud of us getting there and Emily was all puffed up and as proud as I was. Em, who was three and a half years younger than I was. Still, even today, Em is way more scary than I am. She still thinks the bogeyman is going to get me—even after her husband Zero (bless his heart) has installed three dead bolts on this door.

Anyway, that was learning to drive. And that was village life—at least the South Carolina version. This village of ours, McClellanville, didn't have but 400 people living in it. Still, the single main street had five groceries, three hardwares, two drugstores, a hat shop and about six other businesses. Customers hadn't started driving off to the city to shop, but they soon would. The highway was paved by then, and with the proper urging, even a 12 year old could make it out.

To the east was the newly created Francis Marion National Forest and to the west we were connected to the salt marshes and the ocean by a creek that was the harbor. There was an oyster-shucking factory across the street from our house—but it was shutting down, and shrimp boats wouldn't come along until after the war. A couple blocks over were the docks, and we swam there, jumping off the freight boats that brought the groceries in bulk from Charleston. We assumed the creek wasn't polluted but we all had boils from swimming there. Most of the streets were still dirt. Big live oaks, cedars, and palmettos grew everywhere. The houses didn't get painted.

Of course, this is the Great Depression I'm speaking of and nobody had much. Some men were farming and a few lumbering. Jay's father, A.T., eventually became a game warden. He was very good at that—determined and tough. In later years Jay called him "a catcher of men." My own father, Harrington Morrison, ended up building docks and bridges. Our fathers just worked along until they found something. Mama sold milk to our neighbors. We kept two cows that my brother Sonny milked and he delivered the milk. Like everybody we had a vegetable garden, and Daddy brought home seafood and game. Money was scarce.

For social life we had the church meetings, sings, Sunday school and young peoples' groups. Our family was Episcopalian. The priest came maybe twice a month and maybe 10 people attended church. The organist kept playing until she was 102—with my older brother Sonny or my younger brother Horry down on the floor pumping the organ for her. Daddy would fall asleep. All the men did or pretended to. Except one who sat up front and 20 minutes into the sermon would take out his watch and tap the face. End of service.

The young people had dances and parties. Get togethers. We were young ladies by then. The Coast Guard had a station here, and those beautiful boys all dressed up in their uniforms would get off the Greyhound bus. Amy and I would leave the house in our skirts, and then take them off and meet the bus wearing our shorts and showing our nice long sturdy legs.

I did all right in high school. The one memory that sticks with me was being reprimanded by the chemistry teacher. This was probably over a jar of formaldehyde or something because we had no real equipment. Anyway, it was winter and I was walking home, shredding my gloves and crying and wiping my eyes on my sleeve. And Cilla, who was exactly my age, but had taught me to drive, said, "Martha, shut up!"

I shouted, "Cilla!"

She said, "Crying is just what he wants from you. You are not to shed one more tear or say one more word."

So right about then I decided I wouldn't let people like that make me cry. I guess I'd already given up crying to get what I wanted. I'd certainly given it up by the time I got married. There is plenty left to cry about but I set those two reasons aside.

Of course, everything we did bad as children we'd be punished for—except Cilla whose parents would laugh. Her father was a grocer and they could afford to buy her a bicycle. I would walk by her house and think to myself, "It's just leaning on those steps. She's not even riding it. Cilla doesn't really deserve to have that bicycle." Then the next Christmas I got a second-hand skinny-tired bicycle. That was a wonderful present and she and I rode everywhere. We'd go six miles out to the Santee Delta. Then, my friend Jean's father gave her a little blue Ford. The war was on but Jean had coupons from somewhere. We didn't smoke, or drink, we didn't have drugs, but we managed to get into plenty of trouble.

Once Mother and Daddy went out of town, and Cilla, Jean and Amy stayed with me. We had my aunt for a chaperone but the next morning all our friends from high school—including our boyfriends—came to breakfast and we were there in our pajamas when my parents walked in unexpectedly. It appeared that the boys had spent the night, and we all got punished except Cilla.

Now, my granny, who lived with us, was an invalid. She was crippled and later blind, as well. She was in bed in our house for many years, but she was visited often by her Cousin Ethel from across the street and also by her other neighbor Aunt Sadie. They were all great friends and these two would bring all the news of the village with them—except both were terrible recluses who never went anywhere else. I can't imagine how they got their gossip, but Granny passed on all those happenings to the rest of us.

Her husband was called Cousin Dick. He was a strict Presbyterian but a mild mannered man. I recall him playing pinochle in the afternoons, which was a stretch for a Presbyterian.

But the card games that really made an impression were Daddy's Friday night poker games. He had a poker club, and whatever construction job he was on, even if it was in Virginia, he'd be home for that game. There were four or five men his age, but also Wewa Leland and his roommate from Clemson, Wesley Davis, who would eventually be a close friend of Jay and me. Mama wouldn't let me get in sight of these men, but if she was off playing bridge, then I would serve them snacks. They had their liquor bottles out on the table, so I wasn't actually serving them liquor.

I've heard that story about Daddy being frightened of sleeping in the second story of buildings. He was afraid they'd catch fire, so when checking into a hotel, he'd have Wewa Leland who was in his teens, drag along the tugboat's anchor line. Wewa would have to carry it through the lobby and up the stairs to the room so they'd have a window escape route. That may be true.

Daddy was certainly afraid of flying. When my youngest brother Horry got married to Dorothy over in Ireland, Daddy got on the plane with his pockets bulging with liquor bottles. Mother said he disappeared straight into the bathroom and locked the door. He stayed in there and drank all the way to Ireland.

Daddy did love me very much. One of my earliest memories is of him spanking me—but he only spanked me that one time. I had been fooling with the fire in the living room fireplace. I kept poking the logs with a wooden stick and he kept telling me to stop. But I wasn't paying attention. He finally took me out and spanked me. I was very young.

I don't remember ever sitting on Daddy's lap or being hugged or kissed by him. He never told me that he loved me. But he always acted in a way that said it. He would take us swimming or rowing in the boat and always listened to what we had to say. You could tell he loved us, but he wasn't demonstrative. Neither was Mama, but she was still very loving toward her children. Ours was not a dysfunctional family, except that Daddy did drink a lot—but no more than the other men around him. I remember one night he came home from Norfolk, Virginia. I was in the kitchen, but he didn't know it. "Mary! Mary!" The minute he was in that door he pressed Mama up against the refrigerator and gave her the biggest kiss. I was maybe nine or ten and embarrassed, of course. He was always affectionate to mother and they loved each other very much. And we felt secure in that.

One thing that most people don't know—none of my family ever talked about it and the only time I asked Mother she cried and couldn't speak—their first born was a Down's syndrome child. Her name was Mary Oswald and she died of diphtheria. She was badly burned and developed diphtheria. Sonny was just a child but he remembers her. He said she couldn't go to school and Mama was upset over that. He doesn't say more than that and I don't remember her at all. I'm surprised I even know she existed for she was never mentioned.

But it's Jay I want to return to. We hadn't been sweethearts in high school or even when he went off to college. Then he'd dropped out of Clemson College to join the Air Force and had two years in the war—in the Pacific. He'd joined the Air Force and had been sent to Texas. His transfer paperwork fell behind a cabinet and he just stayed playing bridge and doing mostly what he wanted. Finally, he was sent to Hawaii and then to Johnson Island which is far out towards Japan. The island was so small he could see the ocean in any direction from his bunk. He'd been sent there as a radio man who would have to give landing instructions to bombers too crippled to go further. But at the very last minute he got a call from Hawaii. Someone asked if while there he had written a poem and left it in the typewriter. He said he had. They brought him back to Hawaii to be the group's historian—which meant he spent the rest of the war publishing a newsletter, collecting dirty limericks, swimming, and birding. He identified all the birds around him and had a marvelous time.

When he came home from the war, Sonny and I met him at the bus station. Somebody else came along, and Jay and I were in the back seat. We were glad to see each other—but more than glad, it seemed. I'd been writing to Jay while he was gone and I'd realized if I missed him that much, I must really love him and I thought he felt the same way. He had sent me Hawaiian orchids by Air Freight that still had the blooms with dew on them. He had sent a sterling silver bracelet with charms of all the Islands—with a little diamond for Diamond Head. We were in the back seat and all of a sudden he took my hand in his and held it. That was so very strange because we were such good friends—you really don't know how to fall in love with someone you've known so well. We already knew every thought the other one ever had. We were really, really close.

So Jay went back to Clemson College for his final two years. By then, he could have gone elsewhere, but he knew Clemson had some excellent professors and he was more ready to apply himself, as well. After he graduated we got married and moved to the little town of Williamston which was just below the little city of Greenville, South Carolina, where I'd been going to school at Furman.

We rented an apartment from a couple named Marks—the first Jewish people I'd ever known. They were the sweetest couple. They would bring us food. Mrs. Marks thought we had no money, which was true. We had a hundred dollars to start out life with. That got spent. On the day of our wedding, a friend had given us a silver dollar with instructions: "Don't spend this until you have to." I had a job with Traveler's Aid in Greenville. I used that dollar to ride in on the bus and pick up my first paycheck. The apartment was unfurnished. A true cold-water flat. No hot water. We bought a bed and an ironing board that we ate on as well as ironed on. Later we bought a table on the very cheap because one leg was fastened on backwards. But we did have a refrigerator and a stove. Jay said, "One of us has got to learn to cook or we'll starve to death. Since I get home before you, I'll do it." And he continued to cook for the rest of our marriage—at least up there in Greenville.

A very interesting redhead lived in the apartment next to ours. She would come over. Very feminine—very sophisticated. She chewed gum and snapped it all the time. One day I told her I was having back trouble and that I'd never had it before. She says, "Martha, how long have you been married?"

"A month," I answered. She says, "Please don't tell anybody else about your sudden back problem." A learning experience. An etiquette lesson.

Of course, she wasn't the only one offering directions. Jay was having a terrible time teaching. These big high school boys had to stay in school until they reached 16 and went to the mills. Mean. They'd shoot each other. Jay couldn't discipline them. He was scared to death of them. But he did enjoy the few good students he had. He taught math, biology and chemistry—and coached the basketball team. He knew nothing about basketball. They made him the coach because he was tall. And when his team wasn't actually playing, he had to sell cokes to the fans. So funny, all of it. I remember him sitting up in bed correcting papers and one boy had copied a chapter of Shakespeare and turned that in for an essay.

But our real problems were with the school board. The board told us we had to shop at a certain local grocery store. One day this grocery didn't have the instant coffee that we used so Jay dropped by the new Winn Dixie. The coffee was a dollar cheaper. We started shopping there for everything. The board told us to attend the Baptist church. But we rode the bus to the Episcopal Church in Greenville. We both taught Sunday school there. We were burning our bridges—so to speak. The board started rumors that we were having wild parties. We had no parties at all. Once two of Jay's friends from Clemson had visited us for a weekend. And finally the board discovered that I smoked. Actually, I never smoked outside of the apartment. Actually, I only smoked in the back of the apartment where nobody could see. But I guess someone had smelled the tobacco. And I played bridge with the Marks and some of their friends. We weren't accepted there, but we were so very happy with each other.

After one year we moved into Greenville. Jay had two job offers. One was driving a garbage truck and the other was selling debit insurance. Since he couldn't drive he chose selling insurance—which he hated. I already had my job at Traveler's Aid which I hated.

Anyway, even with the insurance job, it would be necessary for Jay to drive and he'd never learned how. He went to a used car lot and picked out a huge old Chevrolet Coupe, which was all he could afford. He asked the salesman to start it. Then Jay got in and put it in first gear. He drove right out and jerked along in first all the way home. He learned to drive juggling the wheel, the brakes and gear shift up and down the hilly streets of Greenville—as he was selling the insurance.

Selling insurance took us over to Fayetteville, North Carolina, where we rented another apartment. Well, up until Jay and I were married, I had never cooked a meal, never ironed a piece of clothing, never made a bed. I'd never even picked up my clothes off the floor. Mama always had servants at the house to do those things and a cook to fix meals—unless Mama cooked. I never did a thing. Emily did. She took an interest in homemaking, but I just spent my time following Jay around in the woods or reading a book. So Jay and I rented this apartment in Fayetteville and one day we came back from breakfast (we had to eat all our meals out) and the woman we rented from was in a rage. She met us on the front porch screaming, "You have the nicest bedroom, the one on the front and look at it!" She made me look through the window. Our clothes and other belongings were strewn all around. Of course, the bed was unmade. She made us leave. I was so humiliated. We found a tiny apartment that really was filthy and I scrubbed it out with a toothbrush. After that I did try to do better. Made the bed up. Took some responsibility for my surroundings. Soon we moved back to Greenville.

This was debit insurance—sometimes called burial insurance—that Jay was selling. He hated that job because he was taking money from people who didn't have it. He didn't actually sell much, either. But he did collect. He collected weekly and chatted with his customers. They would pay along fifty cents or so, but if they missed a payment their policy went back to zero and they'd have to start over. Jay wanted badly just to tell them to drop it. But he had to make a living and eventually he even saved up an entire $300.

Four years we'd been married, and one day Jay came home and said, "Let's start over. We're not getting anywhere. Let's go to Oregon. I can get a job there as a firewatcher."

So we both quit our jobs and took off. Mother looked so sad when she was waving goodbye. Later I asked her why and she said, "Because I thought I'd never see you again. But I knew you were happy and that was all that mattered."

This was 1952. For the trip to Oregon Jay bought us an old Henry J. Kaiser car with four "new" recapped tires—tires that unraveled as we crossed the desert. Jay would cut the unraveling parts off with a razor blade. When we reached Oregon the chief ranger of the forest asked, "You came all the way across the country with those tires?" We said, "Yes." Immediately he bought us four new tires.

But that was at the end of the trip. In order to cross America we had bought a pup tent and air mattresses. Instead of sleeping bags we had army blankets supplemented with white linen sheets and pillow cases—wedding presents. And we had a little camp stove, an ice chest, and a box for groceries.

We were so excited. We were going camping. This was 1952 and there were no campgrounds to speak of. We'd ask farmers if we could park under their trees and sleep. I'll never forget in Indiana we had permission from a farmer. We pitched our pup tent under his tree. But he was plowing his field at night. Forty acres I suppose. In the time it took him to circle the field, we'd go to sleep. Then as he returned the lights on his tractor would wake us. He'd stop and chat for a half hour. Then he'd go around again and we'd sleep for a while longer. A wonderful experience—the entire trip.

When we got to the Red Desert, it turned really cold and the wind blew so hard we had to clutch onto the tent to keep it from blowing away. And at Yellowstone we went to sleep snug in our tent and as usual, our feet were sticking out the end, covered over with plastic— a polyurethane kind of plastic which was new then. The first day of June and we woke up with a foot of snow mounded over our feet. A little cafe was opening up for the first time that summer, and we bought ourselves a meal which was a great extravagance. We had dollar pancakes. Then we just sat inside the cafe and stayed warm for as long as we dared.

Finally, we got to Oregon. We were stationed inland, but drove to the ocean first. Seeing the Pacific I said, "You mean Oregon is on the coast?" That's how I learned geography. Hands on. In the years since we've camped in every state except Hawaii and Alaska. But I must tell you of Oregon in 1952.

The Forest Service people were so very good to us. First we went to fire watching school for two weeks. I went too, because I was to be Jay's relief. Then we were assigned to the Drake Butte tower which was high on a mountain at the end of an impossible road. One or the other of us were to be in that tower during the daylight hours seven days a week.

At ground level, we had a one room log cabin with surrounding windows under the spokes of the tower, and we were to keep watch for fires even from there. Inside were a woodstove and a small bed. Just us. We spent so much time alone together it was like a second honeymoon.

Not long after we got there a letter came from Mother saying, "You've had the trip and now have to pay the price." Lord knows how my letter had given that impression. Jay and I whooped with laughter, and I wrote her back: "The 'price' is peace of mind and heart. We love it. You can't imagine waking up to a cool, brisk summer morning with the birds singing all around, the ground squirrels and chipmunks begging for their breakfast and miles and miles of rolling mountains for a view. Soon the fire is going in the friendly woodstove and the bacon and eggs smell like heaven. There's enough to do during the day to keep you busy and happy but no real worries. In the evening you walk around in the beautiful forest and stop to look for arrowheads, agates, or small wild flowers. You watch the sunset behind Mt. Jefferson and there's not another sight like it in this world."

Still, I wasn't telling her the complete truth. For one thing up there that summer, Jay and I were nudists. We didn't wear clothes unless we heard a truck coming up the road—and that was easy to hear. But one day I was up in the tower and Jay was down below completely naked and cutting wood. I had taken clothes up with me in case anybody came.

Well, I saw a rancher coming up on horseback and I yelled to Jay. This rancher stayed to visit a bit. We wanted to be hospitable so I learned to make upside-down cake in the frying pan. Other ranchers started visiting, too. I'd serve cake and coffee. This was unusual. Usually the firewatchers were ignored. But they brought us venison and antelope and we were glad for the company.

On Saturdays and Sundays I had to go up in the tower. On the other days I would get up and start the fire in the woodstove and then carry the little gas heater to the outhouse that sat on the side of the mountain. Not quite like I'd told Mama, because even in summer it could drop to 18 degrees at night. On the weekends Jay would tell me to stoke the stove and I'd push him out of bed—since "I" was on duty then.

On weekdays, I would sit outside with nuts, berries and the like in my hand. I'd just hold the food and sit absolutely still and animals would come. First I'd put it out on the rock and then I'd move closer. Finally I'd hold the treat in my hand and the Clark's Nuthatches, scrub jays, other jays, even chipmunks would eat from my hand, and little ground squirrels—like little people—and red squirrels.

When we'd first arrived, I'd shouted, "Jay, look at that! That is the most interesting bird." Of course, I'd never seen anything like those Western birds. But he said, "Mart, that's just a robin, a robin exactly like ours." I said, "Well, it surely does look different out here." These birds eating out of my hand really did look different, wonderfully exotic—and not one was a robin.

That summer I had the kind of leisure I've never had since. Jay would be in the tower. I'd bake my cake and wash the windows. After that there was nothing to do but read. I'd take my book, my *Moby Dick*, and sit on a rock. I'd feel that warm sun on my back and arms, forget about the reading and just gaze at the mountains. We celebrated our fifth wedding anniversary at that fire tower in Oregon and life had never been so good.

The nearest town was Prineville. Close by but still several hours away. The roads were awful. With ruts a foot deep and boulders protruding, some of those roads were no more than glorified stream beds. Jay would drive to town one day a week to do our laundry and buy some groceries. Ordinarily I'd call in a grocery order and they'd send everything on Friday. But I hated to call in my grocery list. They laughed at my pronunciation (my Southern drawl) and when I ordered "hominy" meaning "grits" they sent canned hominy in lye.

Anyway, Jay had gone to town one Saturday and I was in the tower. Over the radio I heard somebody say, "Did you get Shuler out?" Somebody else said, "Shut up!" Of course, I called in and one of the rangers explained that Jay was coming home and stopped to take a photograph on the side of the road. "When he pulled back out," the man explained, "his tire was too close to the cliff and he sort of went down it. But he is all right. We got him out." The car slid down the cliff and rested against a tree. Jay climbed out the window and scrambled up to the road. He got home but he was awfully late.

And that accident at the cliff was how it would be from then on. Really. The worst accident he had was in Mexico. Climbing a tree to photograph a bird, he fell and broke his ankle. And a lot of the time the accidents weren't even accidents. Wherever we went Jay had a habit of lying down on the roadside on his belly to photograph tiny little flowers. Inevitably somebody would stop and want to know if they could help—for they assumed he needed first aid. And one man even said, "I'll help you get him back in the car and I've got coffee here."

We stayed on at the fire tower from early June until snow fell. That's how our contract read. But once the snow started we had to get off the mountain immediately. By then Mother was with us. At the end of July I had started begging her to come and the first of October she'd arrived. She had flown out to see us and to make the trip home. We planned to stay in different parks.

We were already packed, but even so the weather got bad quickly. Just that narrow dirt road going straight up from the bottom of the butte. Jay was outside the car, holding it on the road with his hands and shoulder. I was steering the Henry J. and Jay was using his body to keep us from skidding and plunging to our death, and halfway down, Mother shouts, "Martha, you forgot your snake!"

And I had. I'd forgotten my Pacific Rubber Boa that I'd always wore around my arm. It loved the warmth of me and was just the nicest snake. This was the one wild pet I would allow into the cabin and the only one I intended to take home. I'd punched holes in the top of a jar and had him in there. We really were attached to each other but being halfway down the mountain, we had no choice but to leave him behind to freeze.

That trip home was wonderful. We still didn't have any real camping equipment. We did use our ice chest and little stove to make meals, but Mama paid for motels all the way home.

Except she only got one room. Mother and Jay loved to stay up all night and talk. Finally, one night, I said, "Mama, you just get in bed with Jay and I'll get in your bed. I can't sleep with you all talking and laughing all night long." Mama had such a good time on that trip. Daddy would never go anywhere but he was happy to send her. We went to the north rim of the Grand Canyon, Carlsbad Caverns—we went to every park we could.

That was Oregon. That was my first experience of just trusting Jay completely. I always had this dark vision. I worried about everything. But that trip changed our lives.

I never felt the same about anything. I saw life was to be lived—to be experienced with joy. We—that is mankind—weren't meant to work 9:00 to 5:00. But if we had to, at least, we could pick jobs that allowed us the summers off.

And that's what we did. After that, each summer we'd take off to Wyoming or the Blue Ridge Mountains. We'd go somewhere.

And sometimes we didn't even wait until summer. We just went. After that summer our lives changed completely. My husband Jay became a nature photographer. Oh, Jay saw beauty everywhere. He would say, "Mart, look at this..."

(Doe Hall, S.C. 2000)

Chapter Two

My husband Jay became a nature photographer.
Oh, Jay saw beauty everywhere.
He would say, "Mart, look at this...."

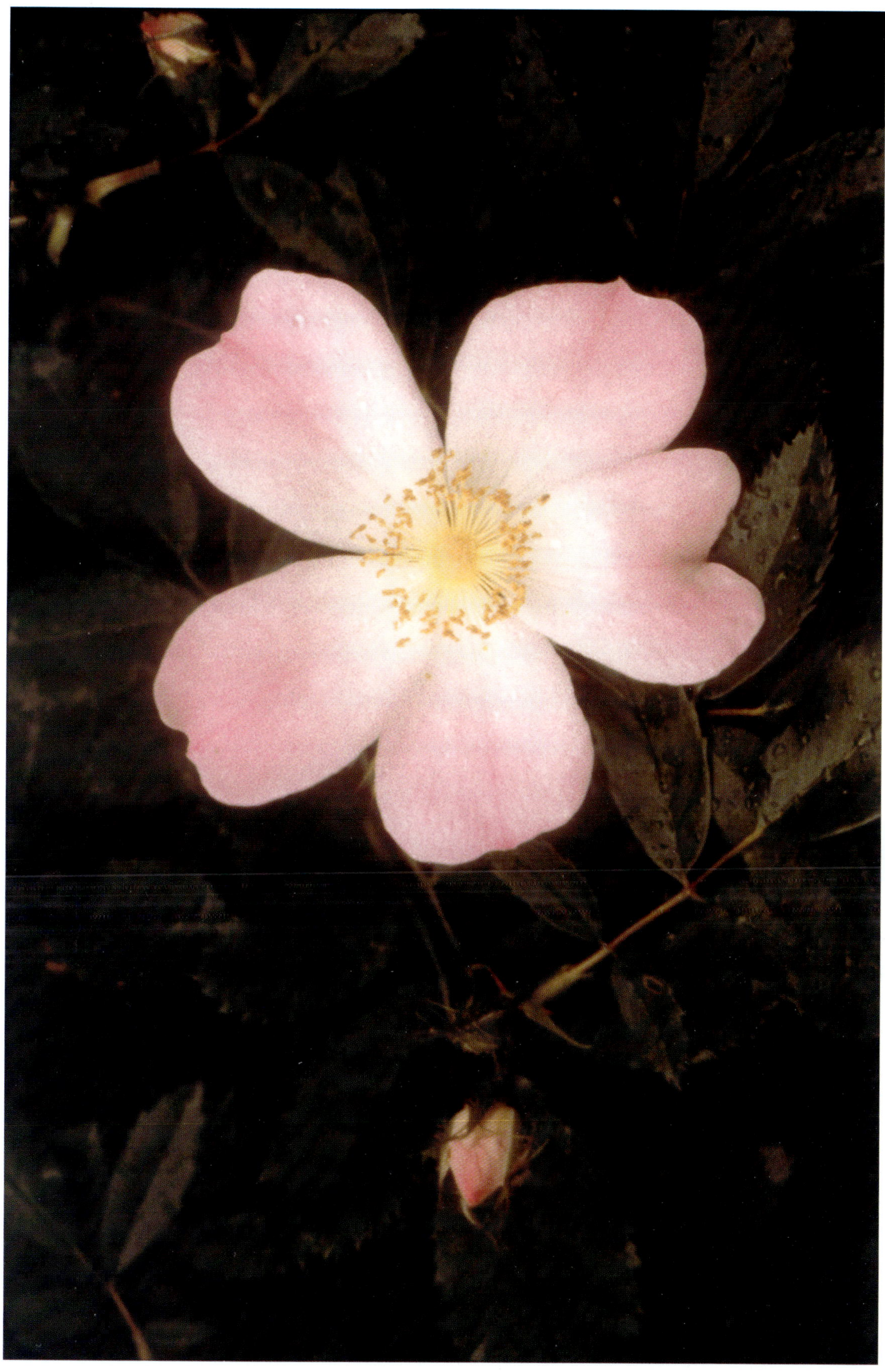

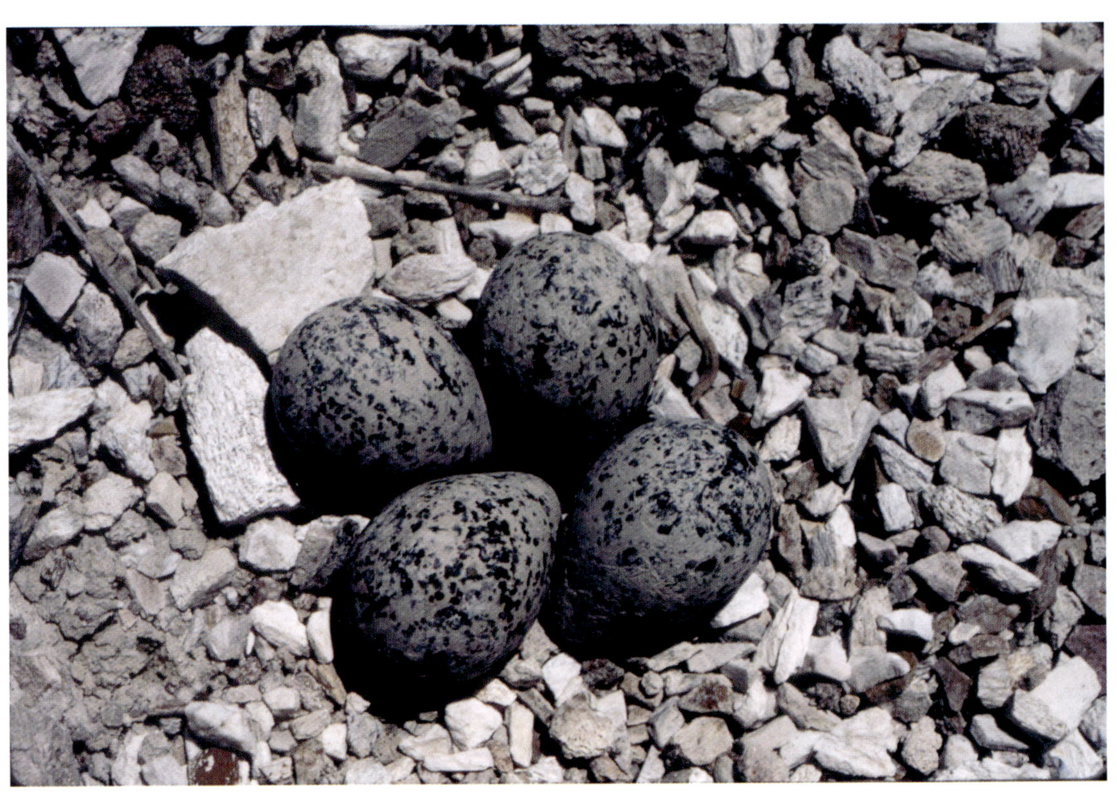

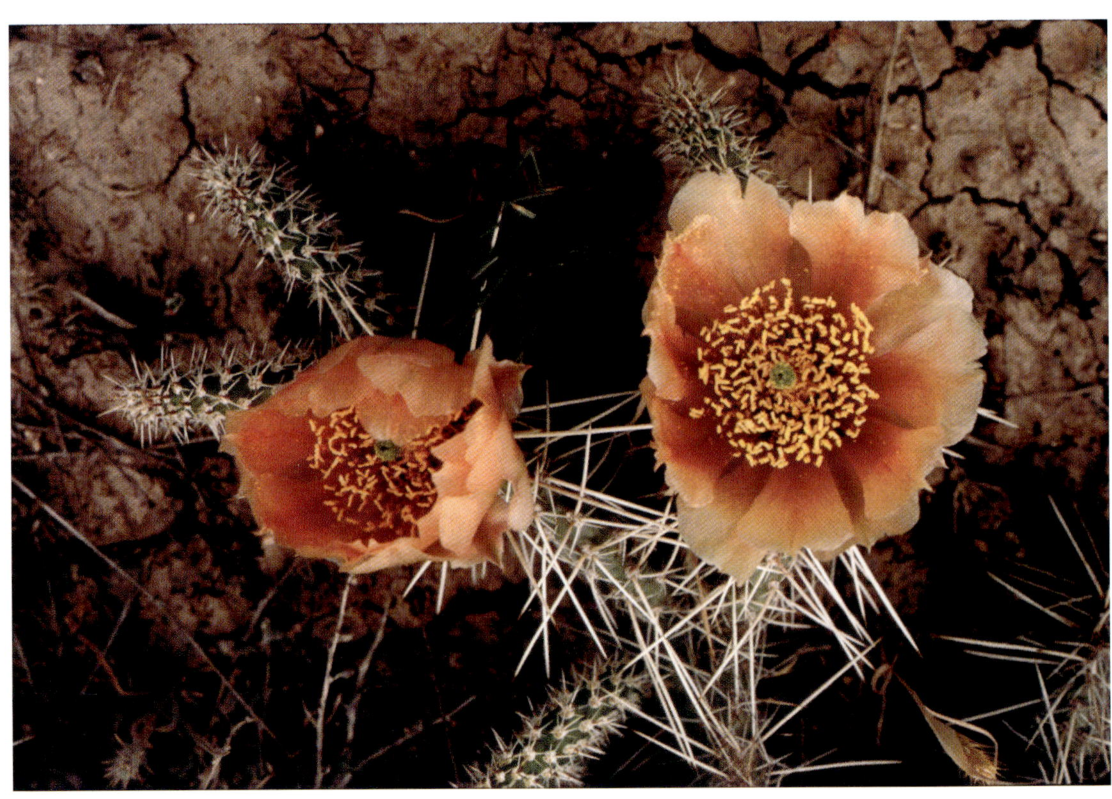

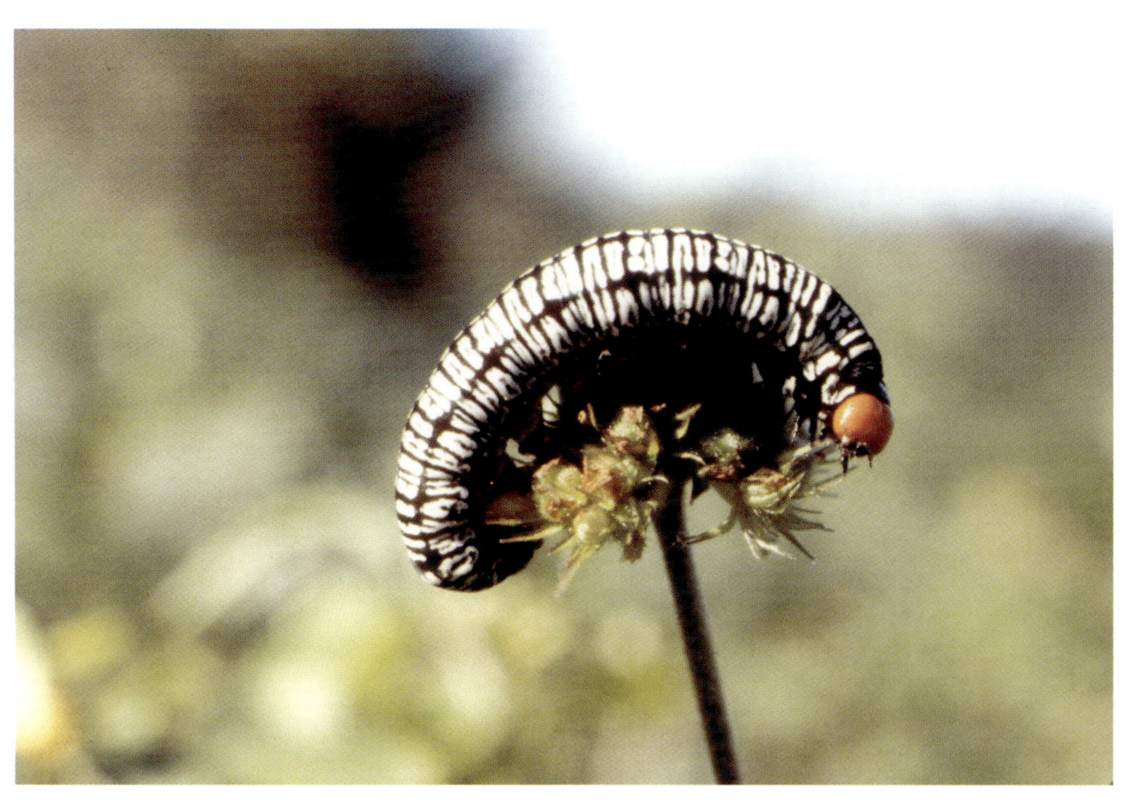

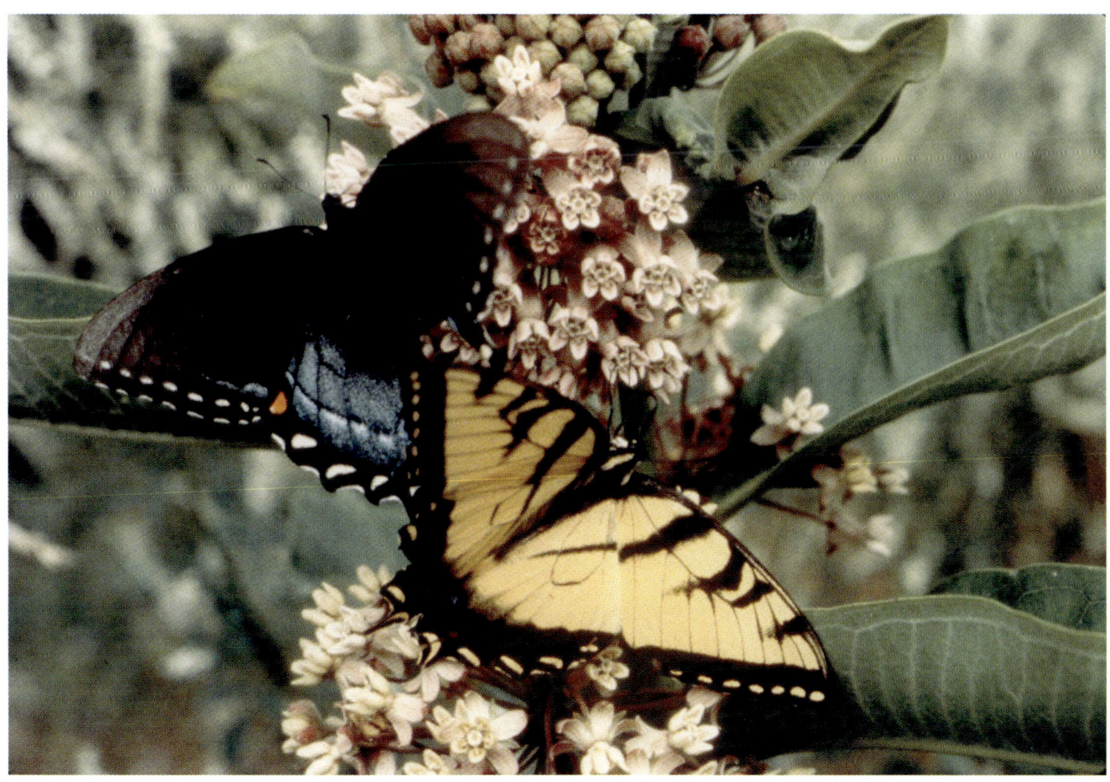

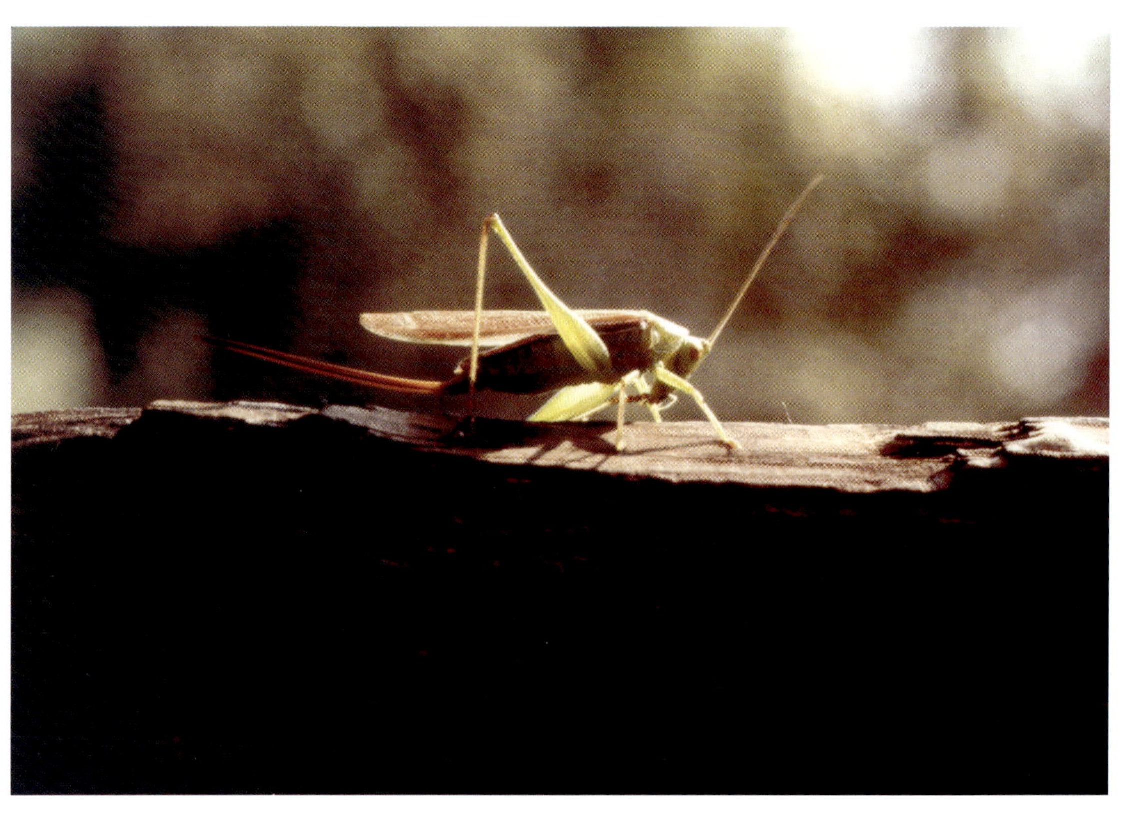

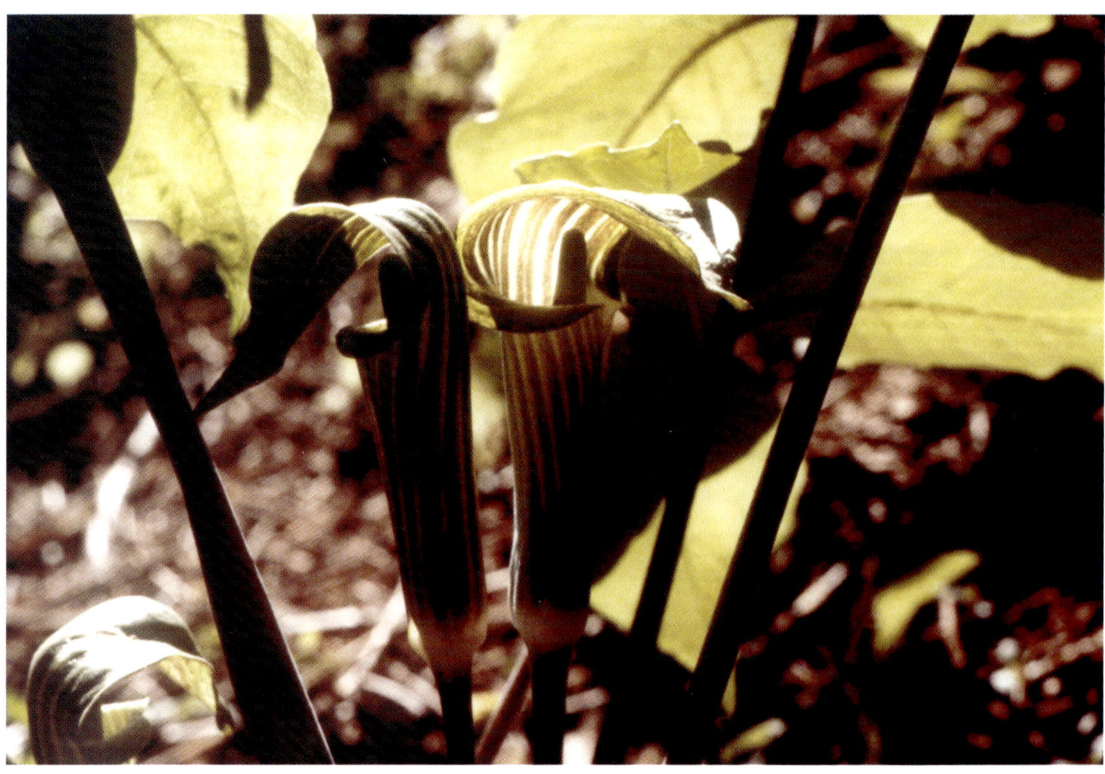

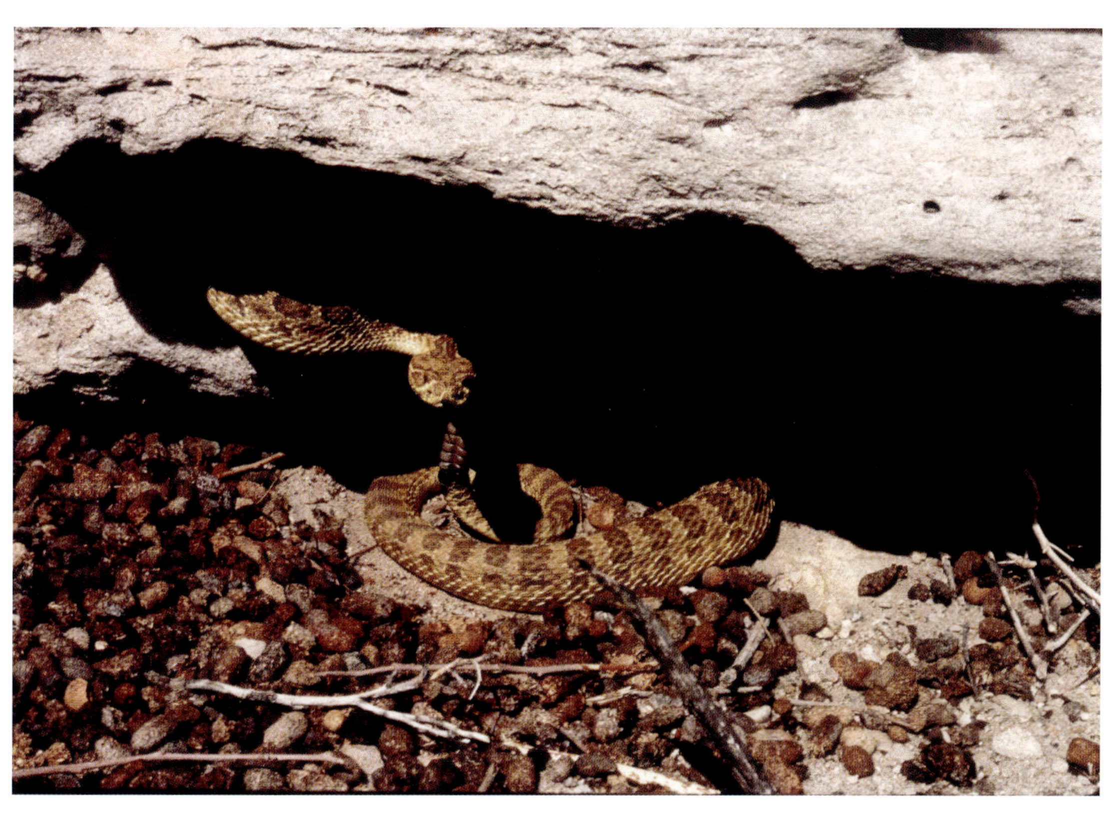

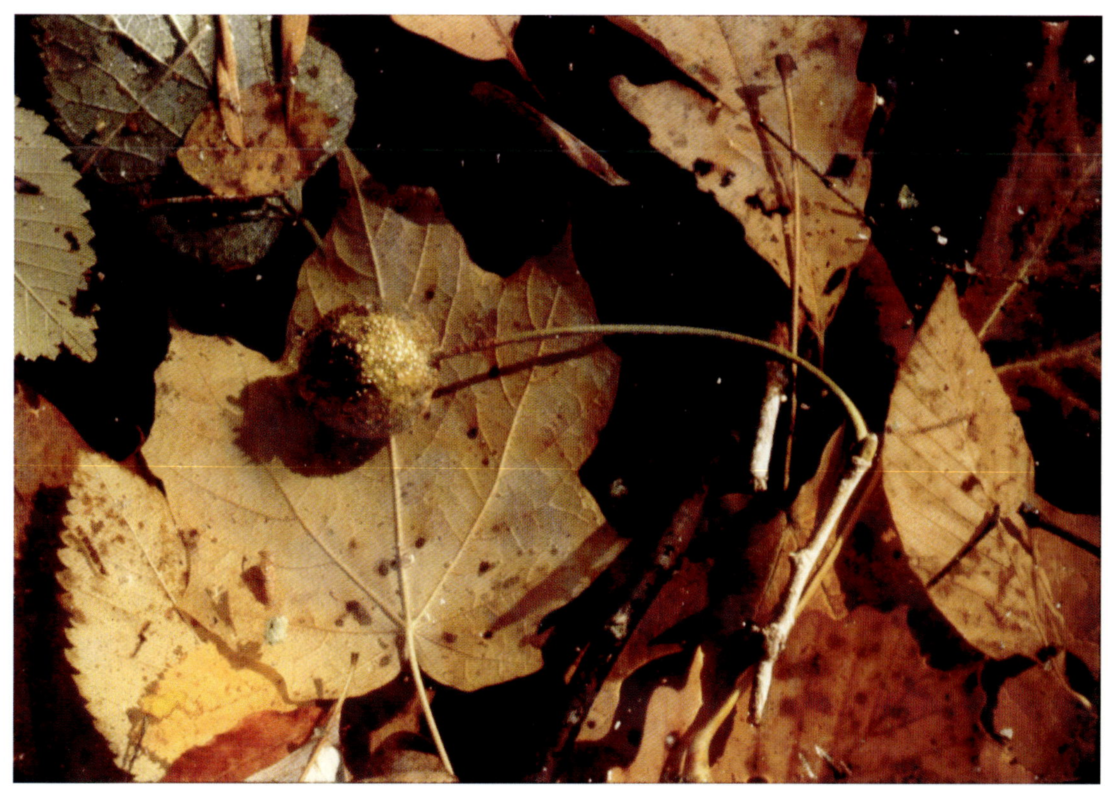

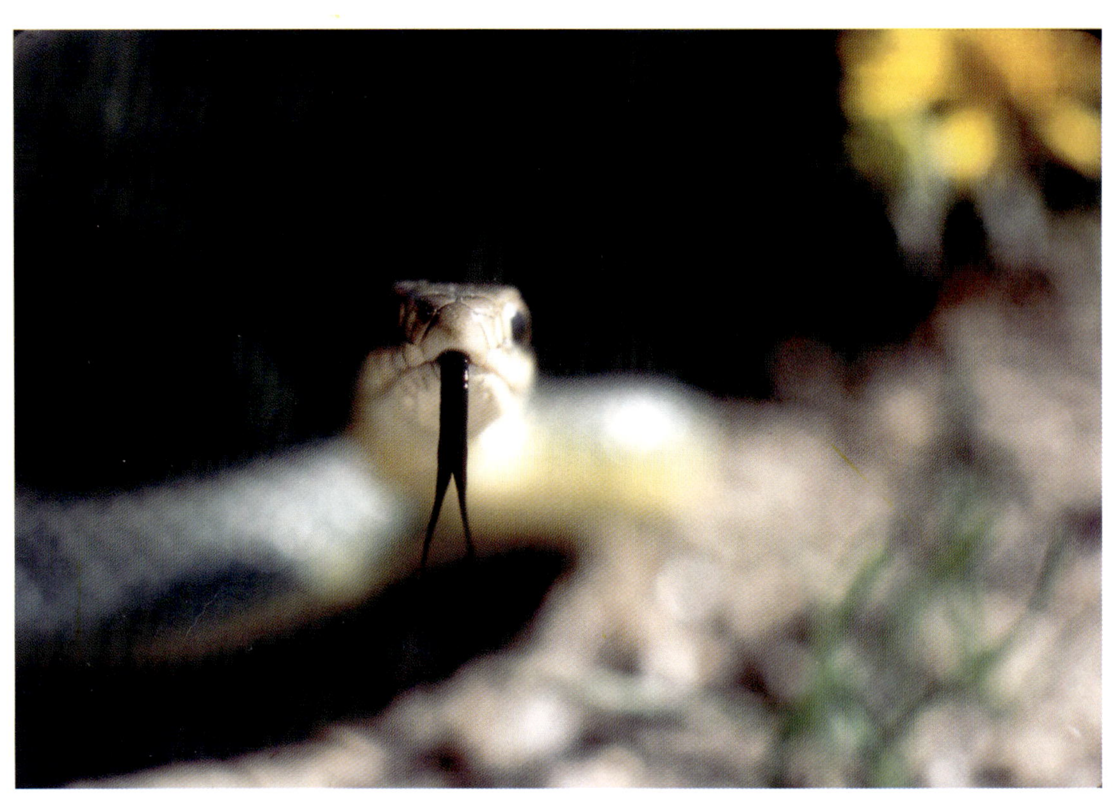

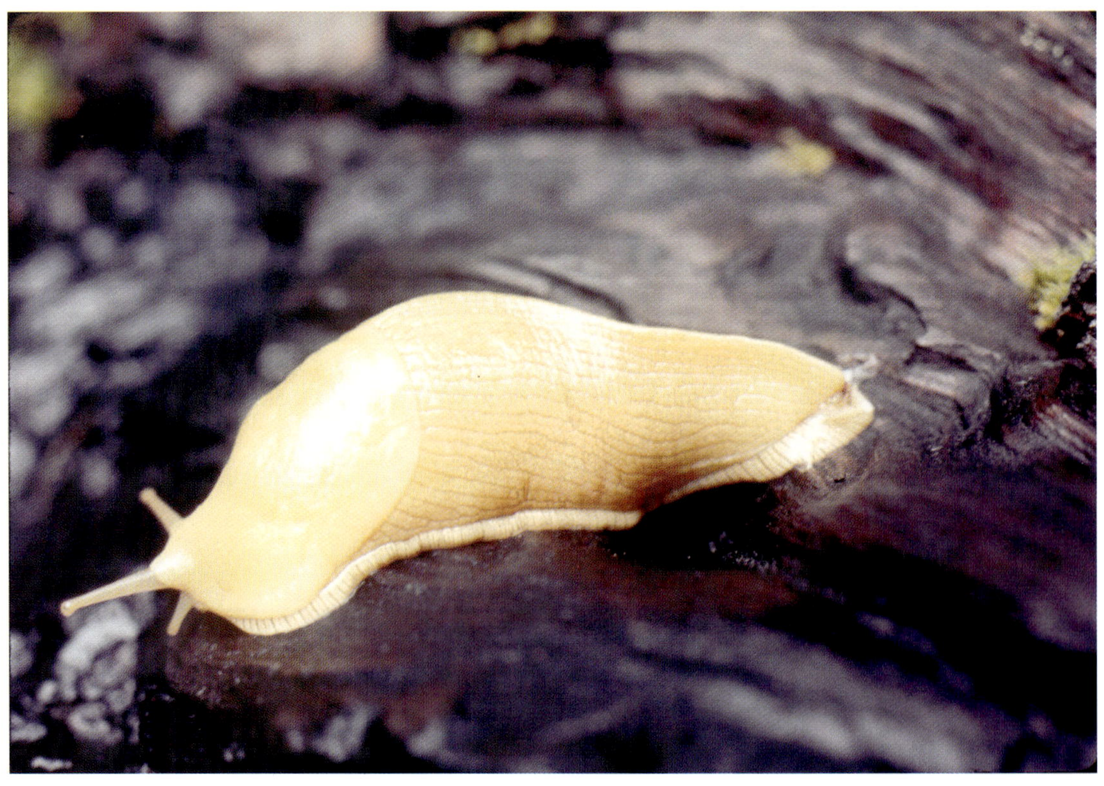

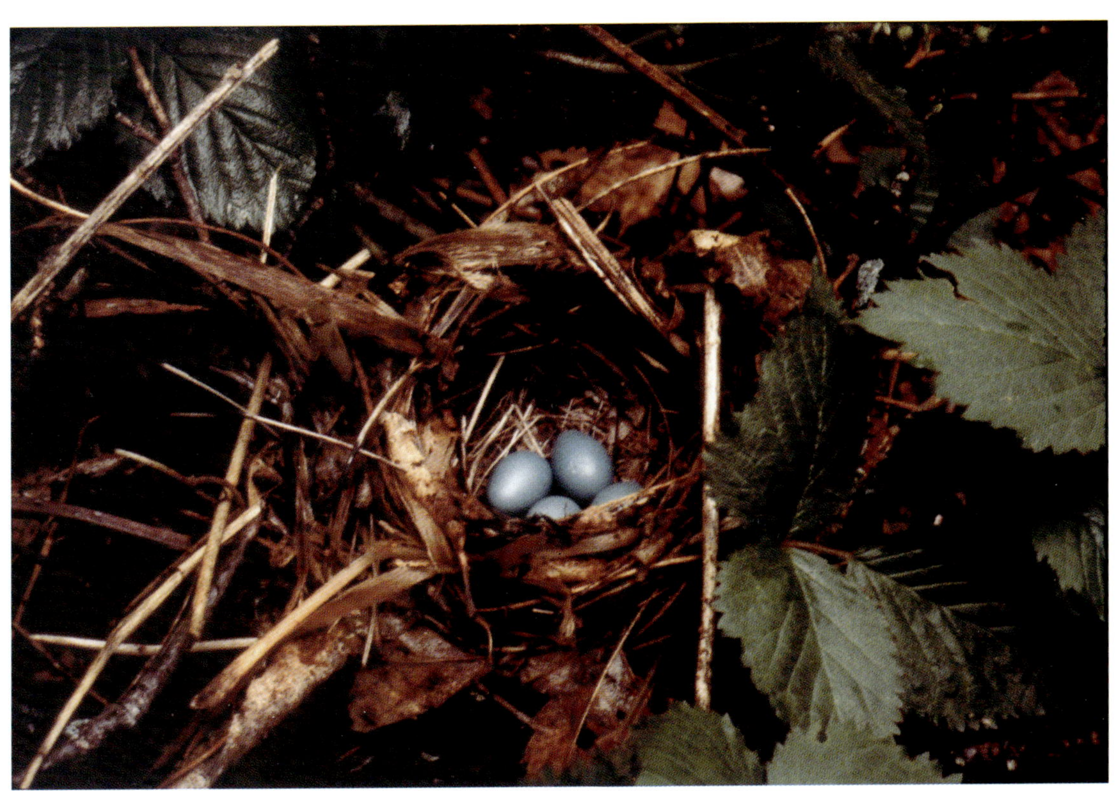

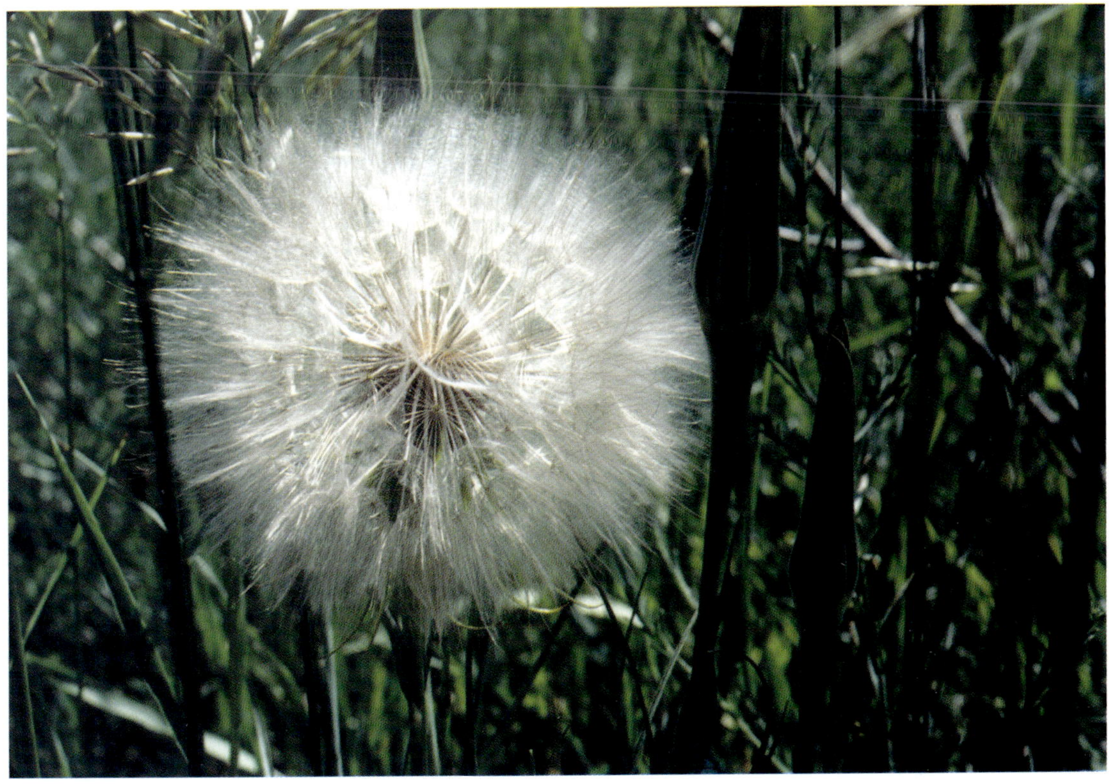

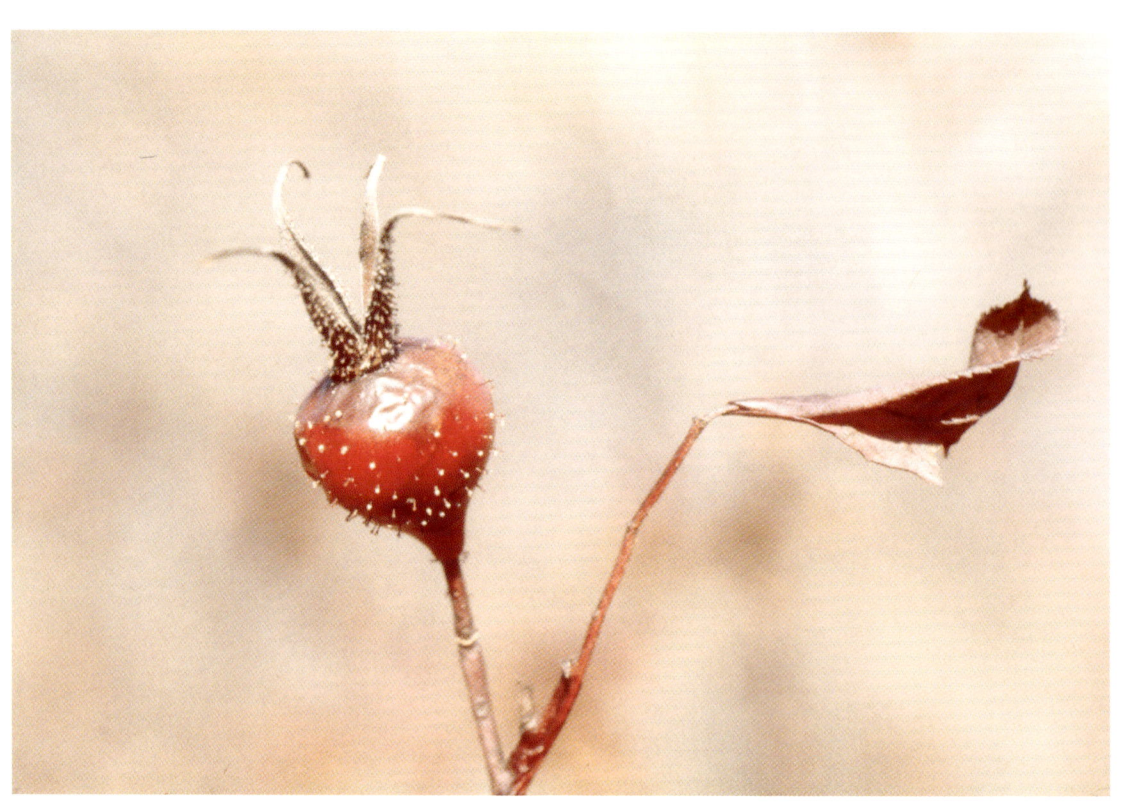

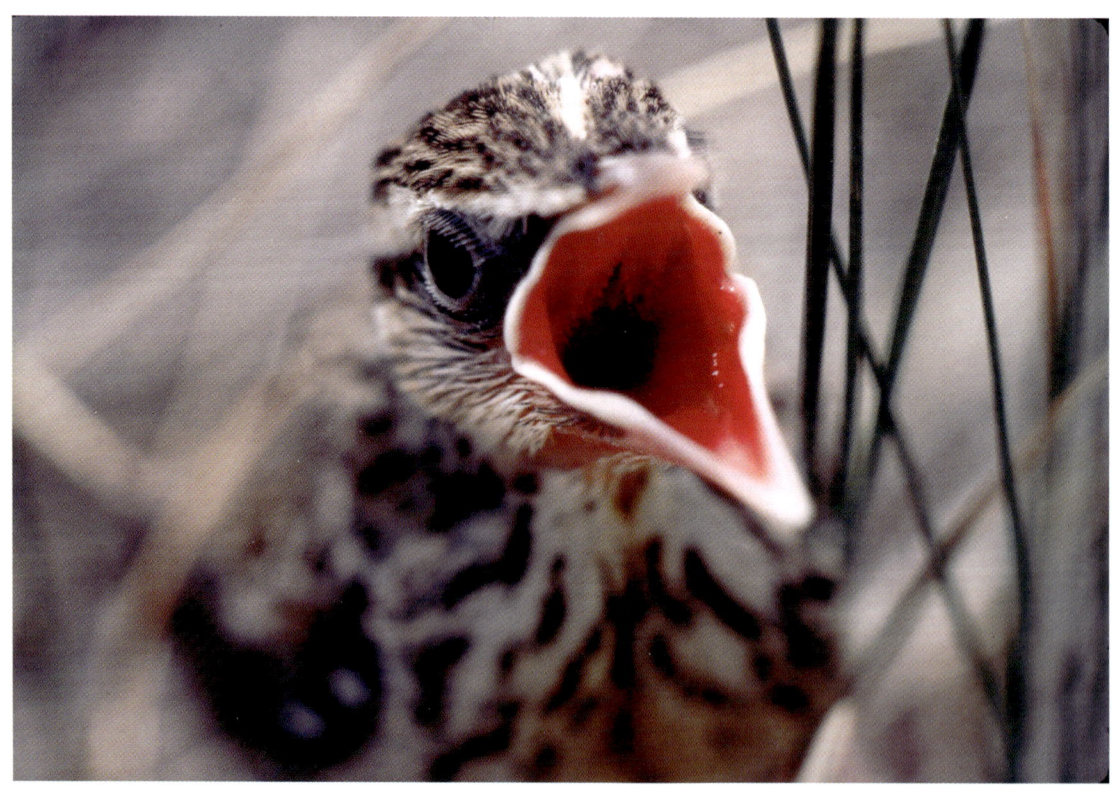

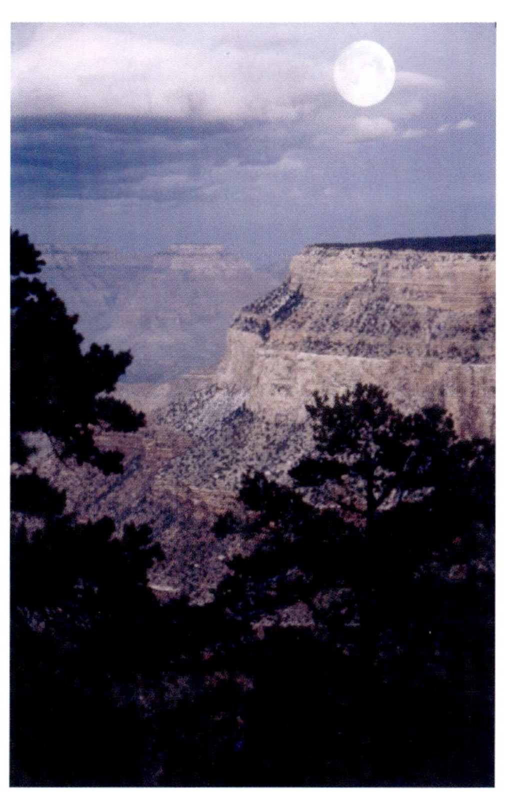

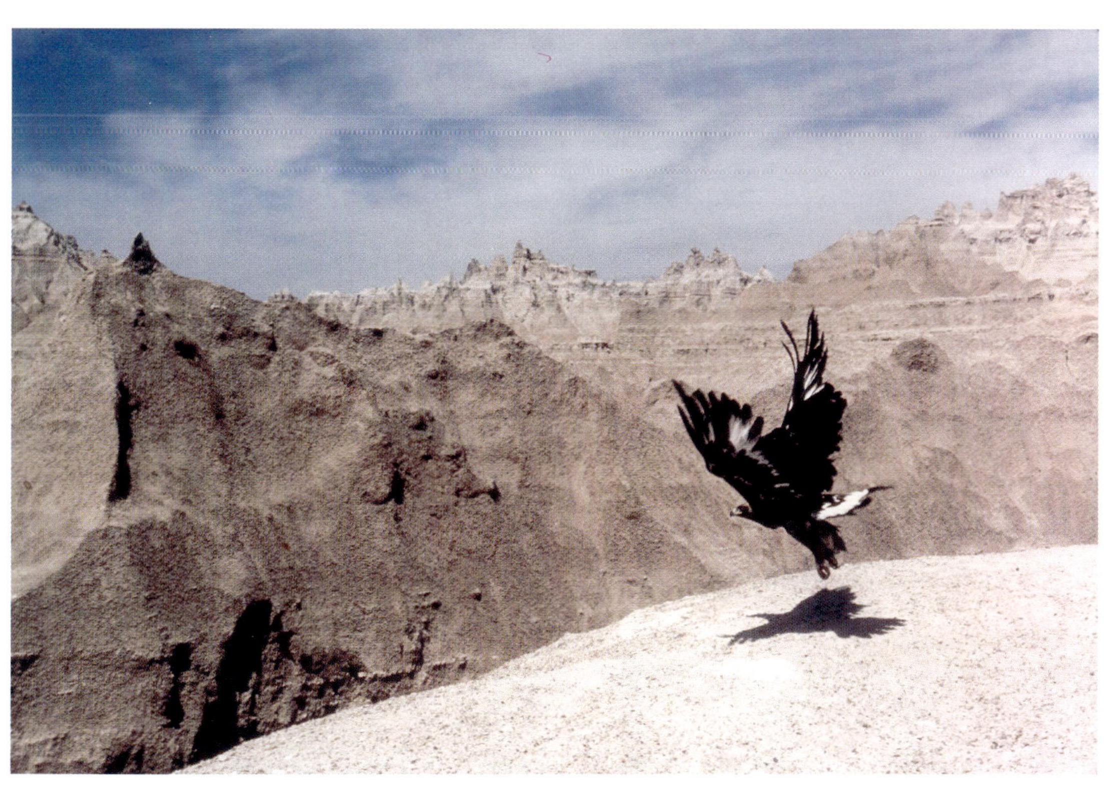

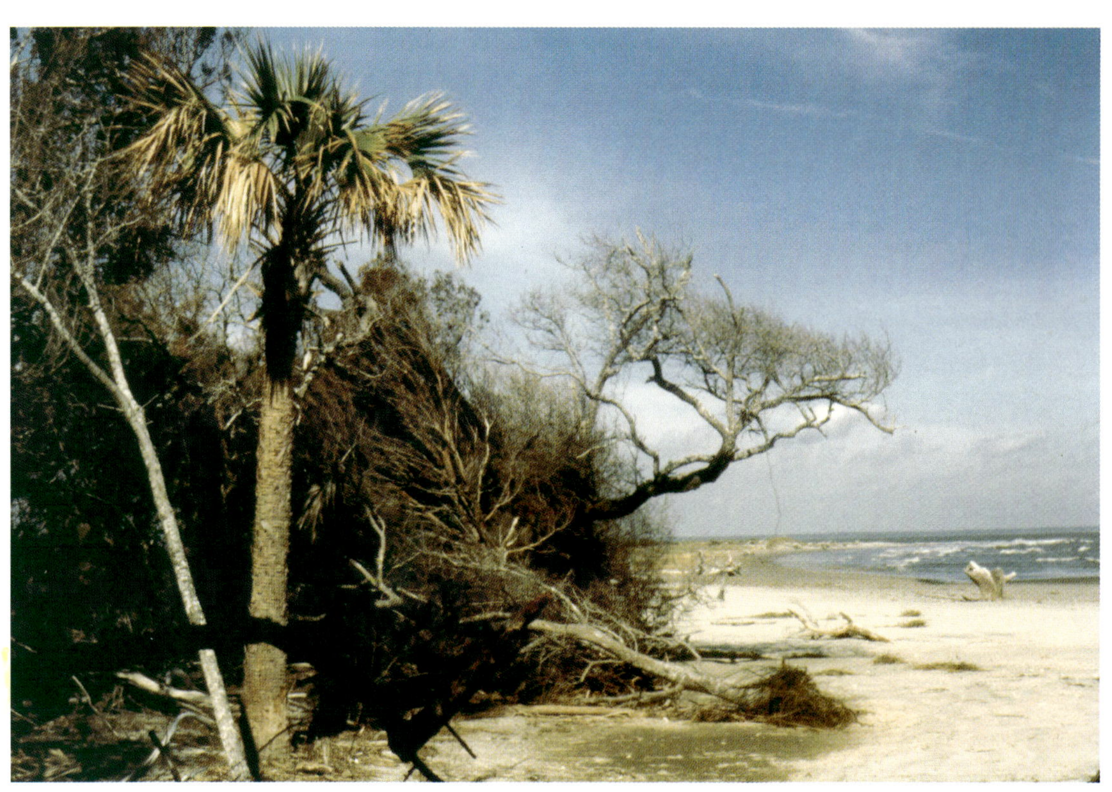

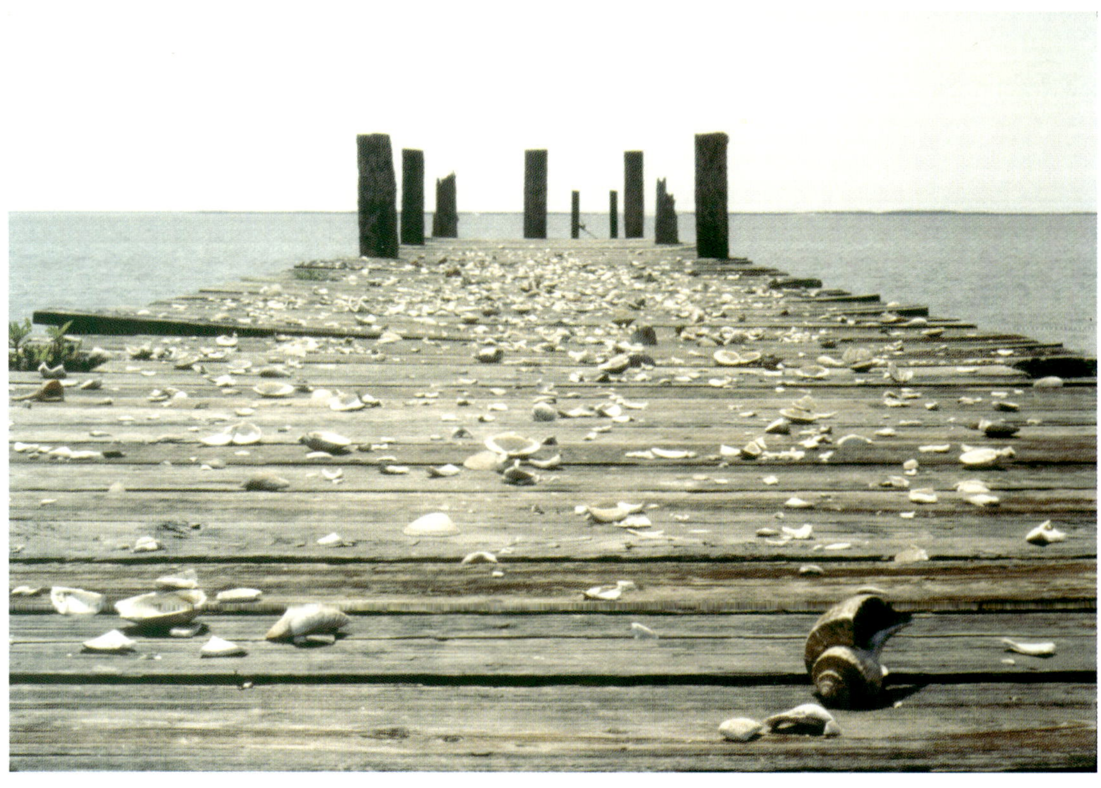

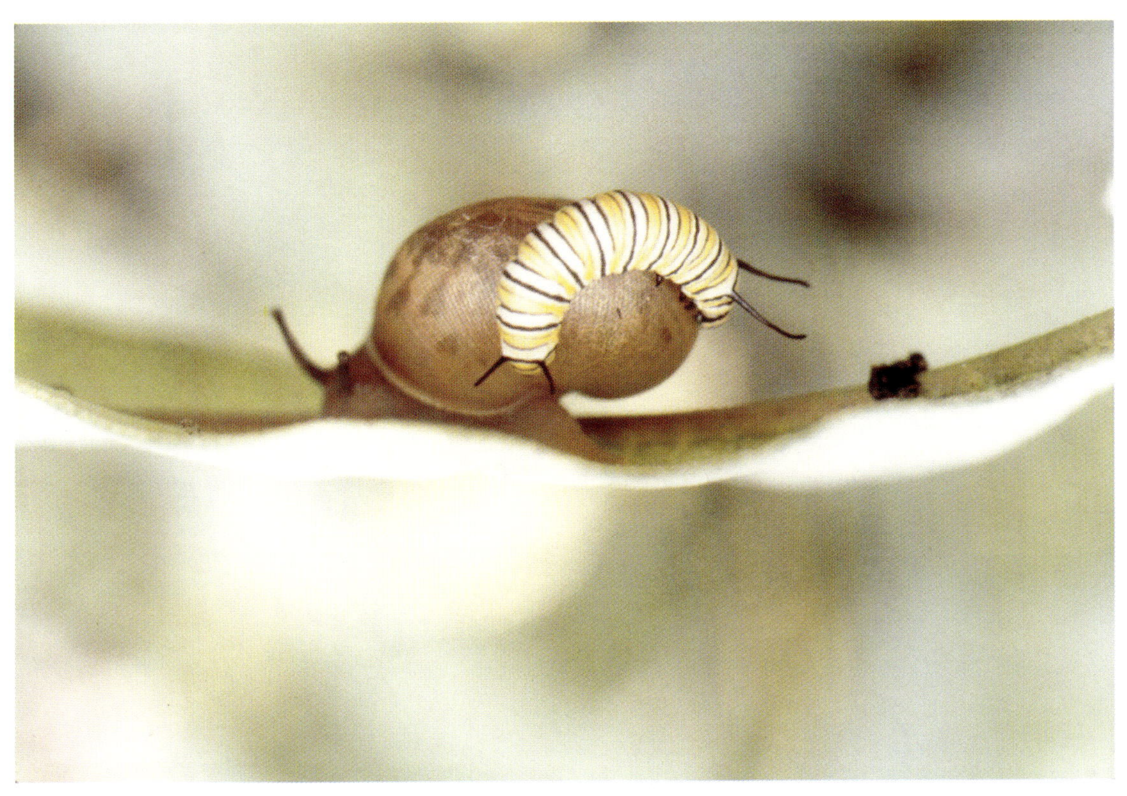

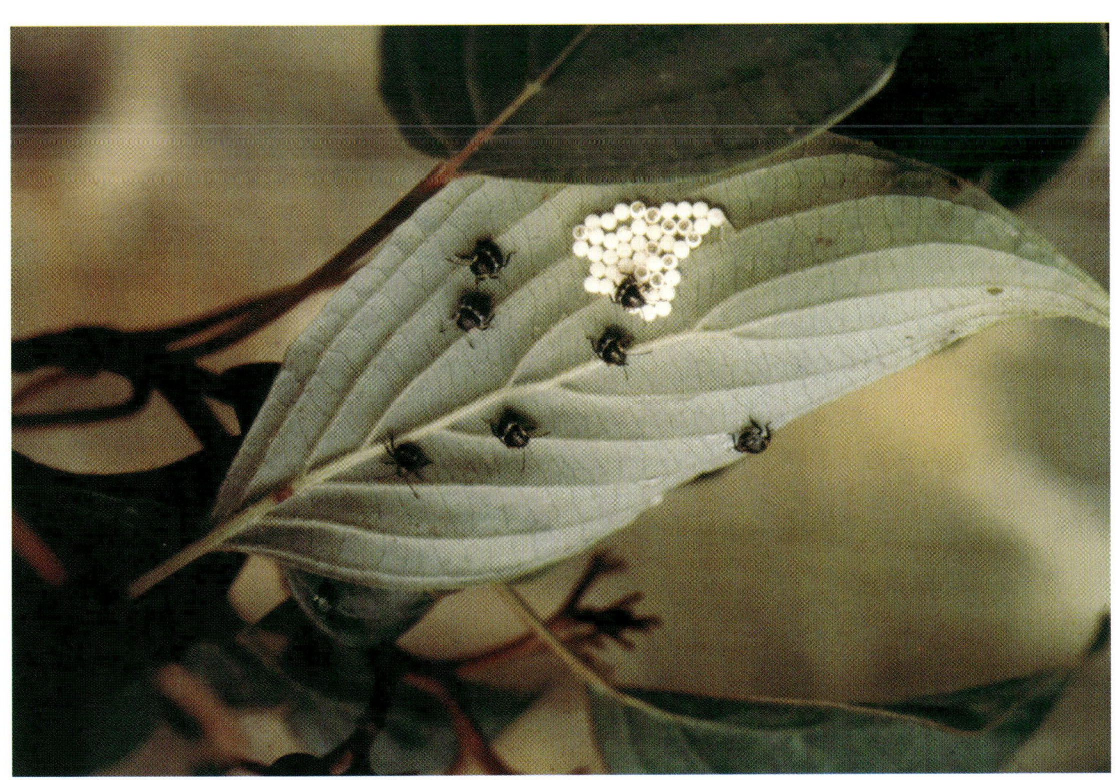

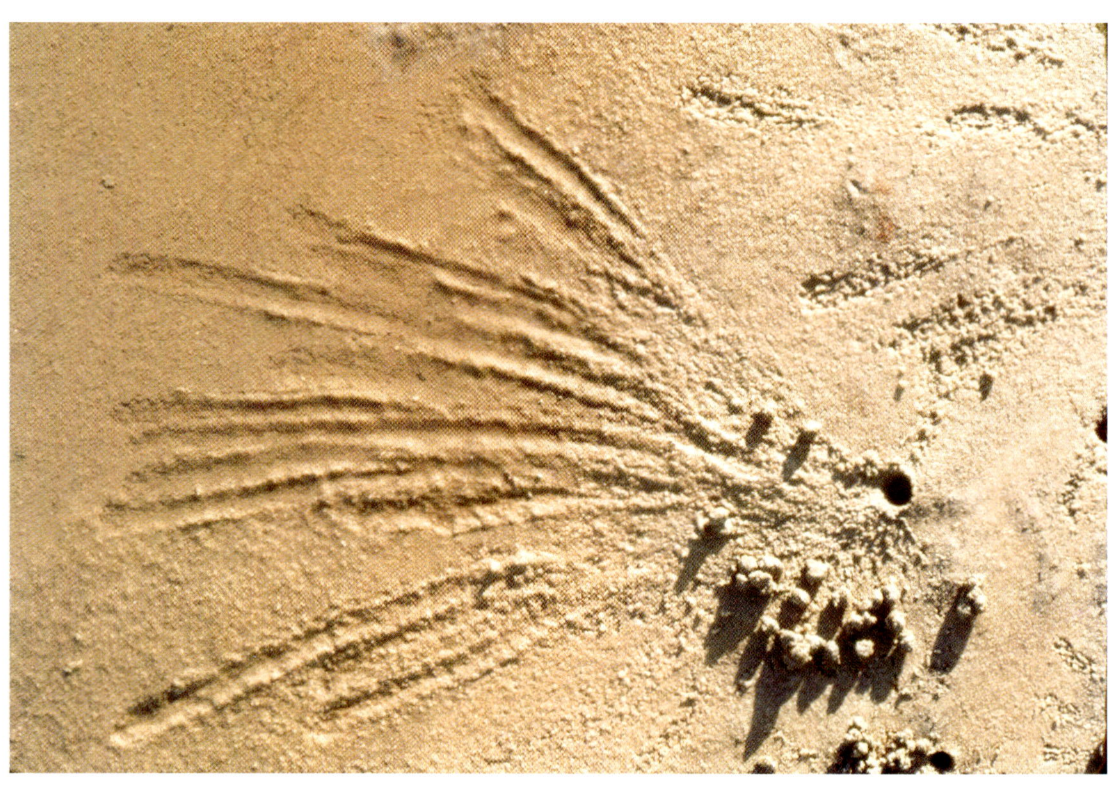

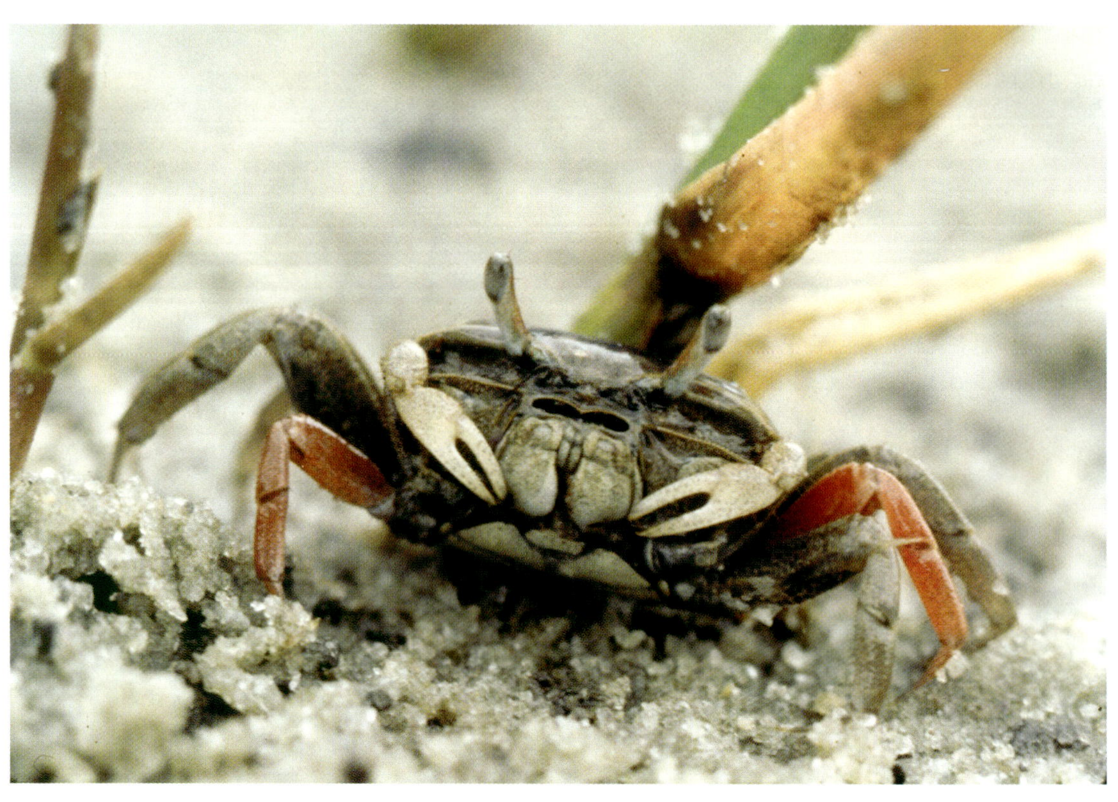

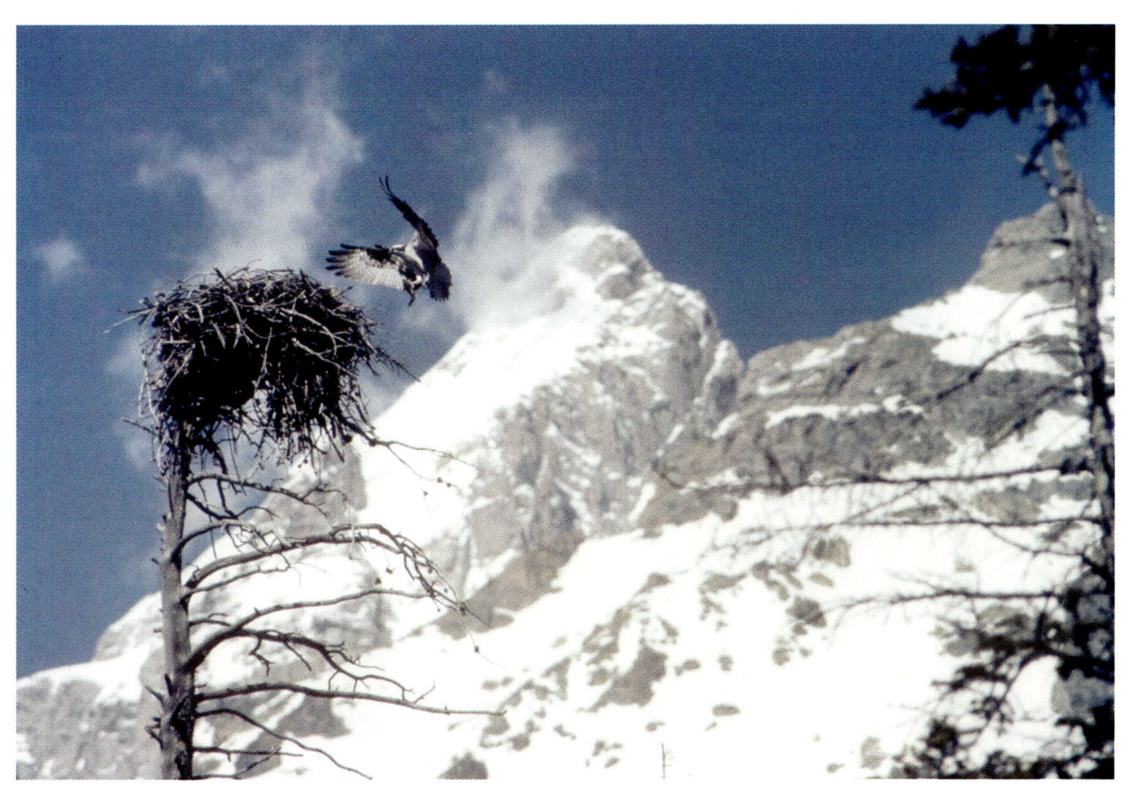

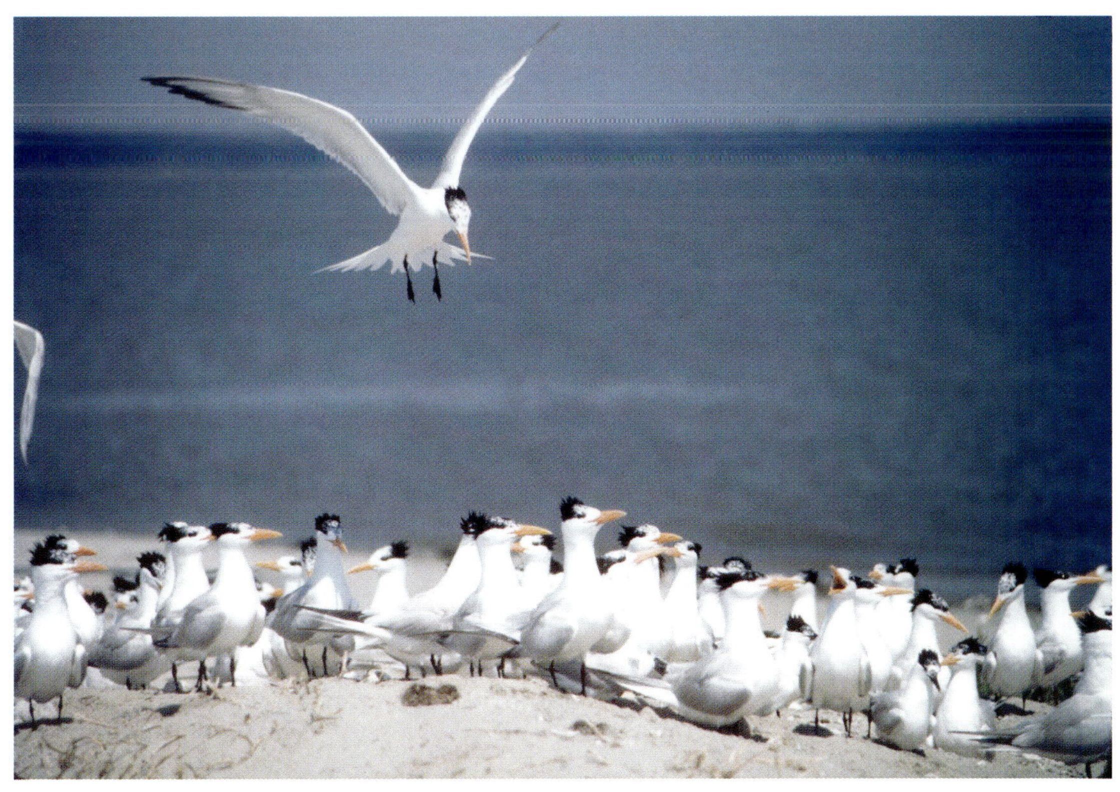

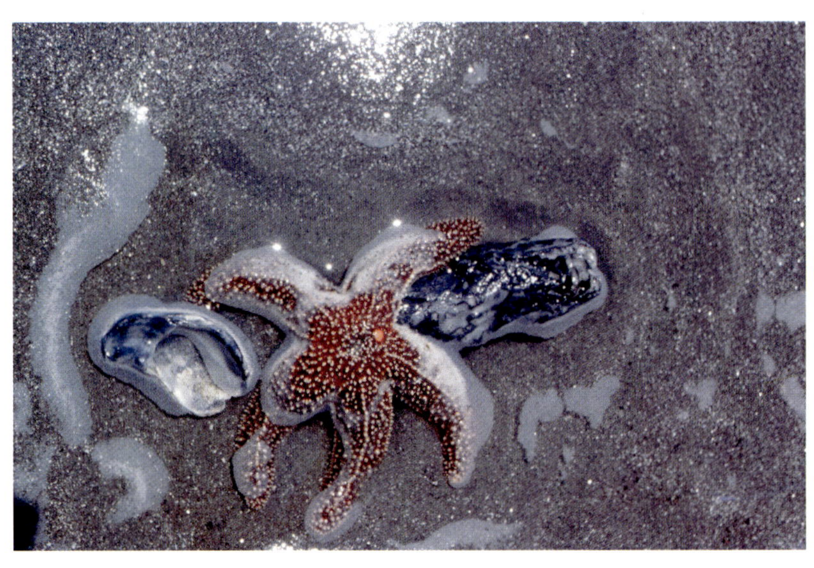

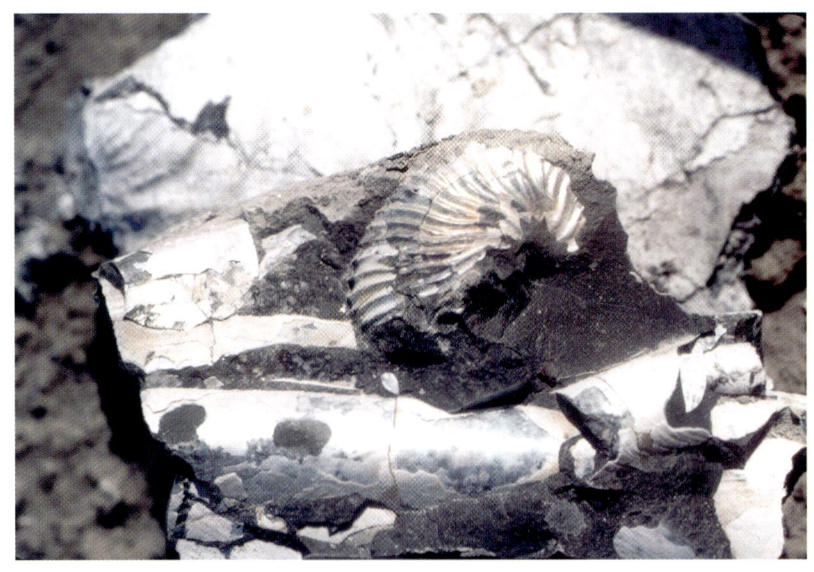

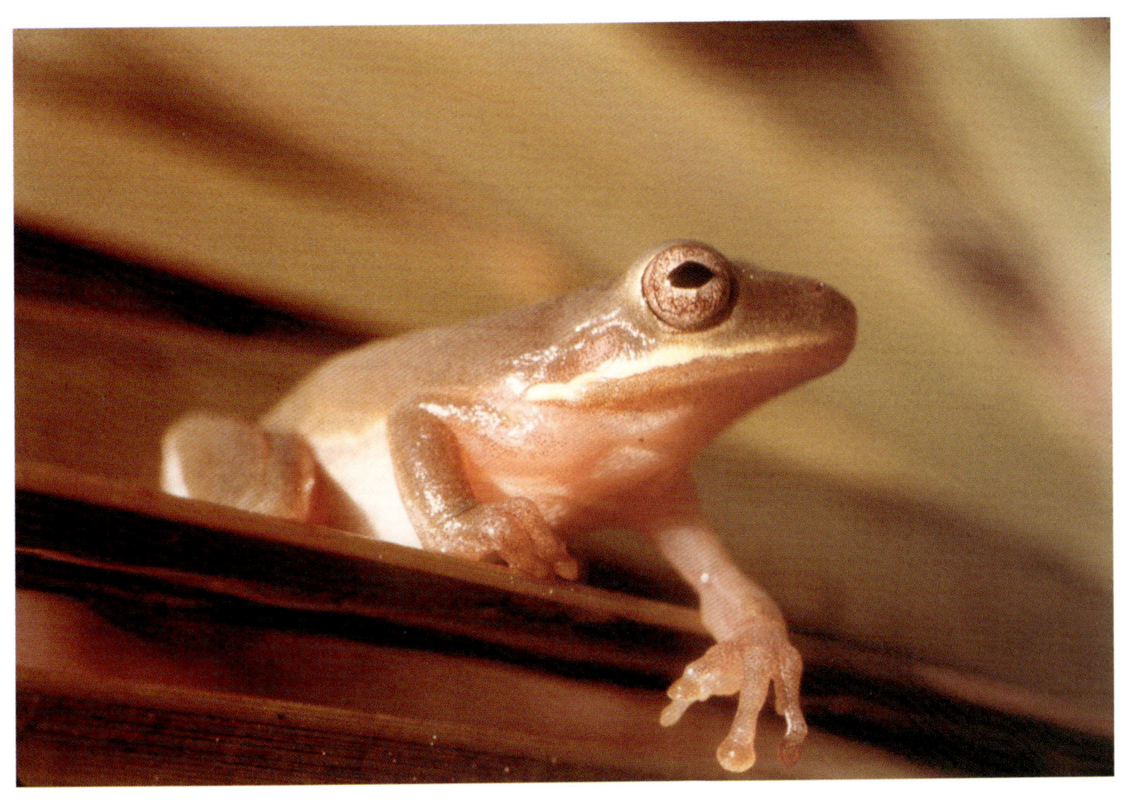

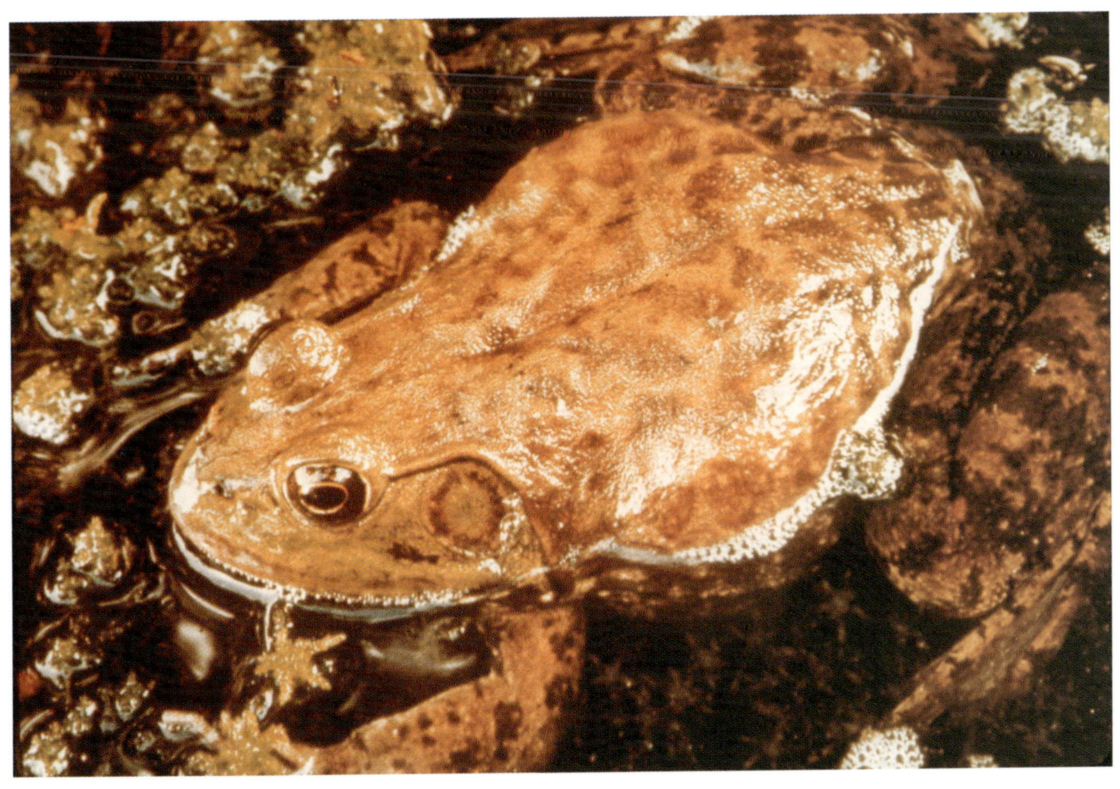

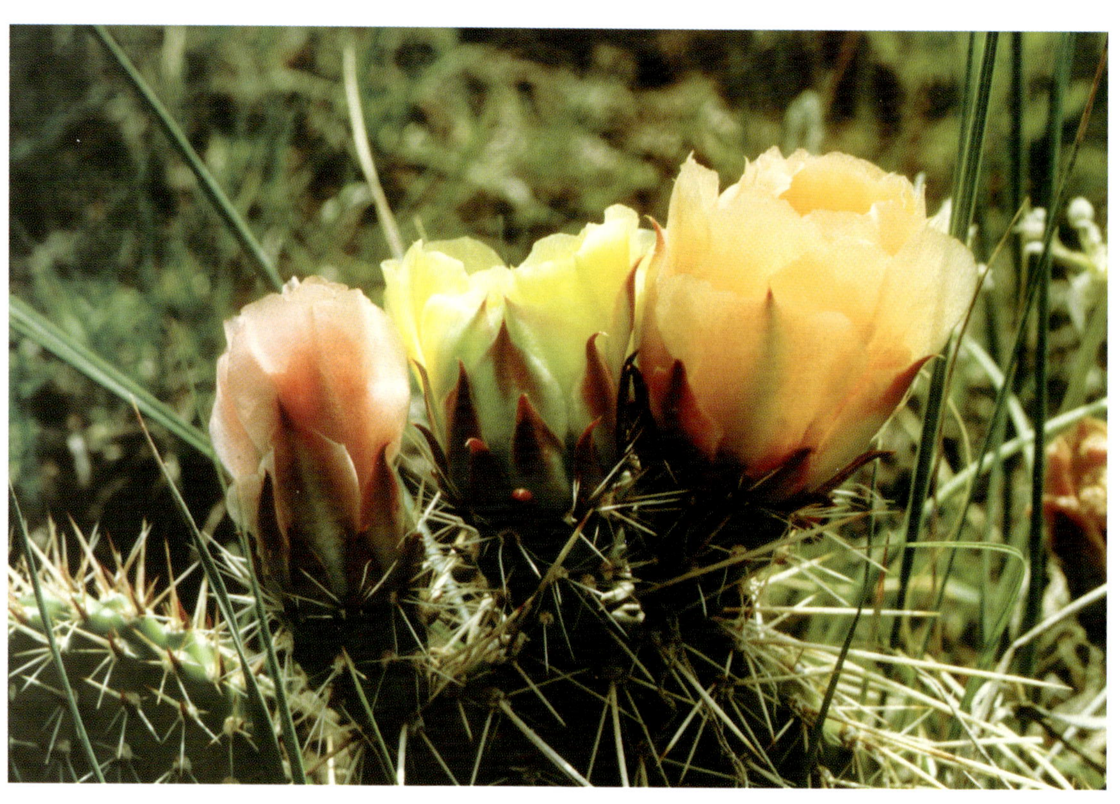

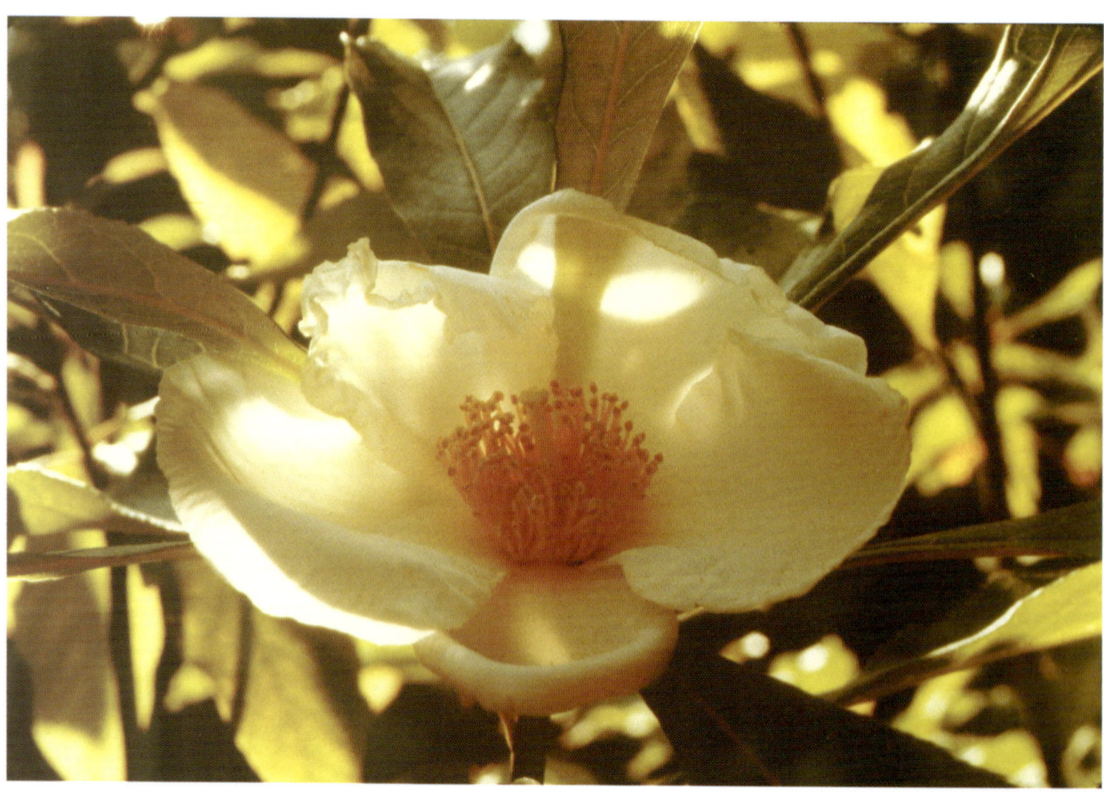

Chapter Three

Our Lives Together

Martha: To give you a taste of our adventures, I'm jumping ahead. These essays of Jay's and the ones in the chapters that follow first appeared in Greenville, South Carolina's newspaper, The Greenville News. His weekly column was called "On Nature's Trail" and ran from 1969 to 1973.

JAY: On Traveling

New Hampshire

We thought spring had run out of gas on the New Jersey Turnpike, but apparently the entire season had slipped quietly inland over the Catskills and into the valleys of Vermont and New Hampshire. What we took to be a wintry landscape was the sick earth, poisoned by the great city—a belt of desert around the metropolis much like the vacant medium Sir Arthur Fleming observed around spots of penicillin mold.

Turning west just below New York City and then moving north, we soon saw hillsides with shadblow in blossom and, flourishing in the bogs, marsh marigold and skunk cabbage. Though 800 miles lay between us and our home in the Carolina foothills, many of the early spring flowers were familiar. There trailed Spring Beauty, the same sweet scented flower blooming a few weeks ago on our Glassy Mountain. Martha pointed to a clump of *Trillium erectum*, its maroon petals lightly touched around the edges by frost. When she stooped to sniff one she found that it deserves its New England name—"Stinking Willy." *Trillium erectum* of the Carolina Blue Ridge has no odor our noses can detect.

Everywhere we looked the lines of Robert Frost came to mind. As if we were turning the pages of his book and finding all the poems—but in a different order. While birches were leafing out, some, pulled down by the weight of winter, still trailed their tops upon the ground. Walls of stones turned smooth on the wheel of a glacier, snaked over the landscape. "Something there is that doesn't love a wall." Well, New Englanders must love them dearly for they have built them everywhere.

On the top of a Vermont mountain we came upon banks of melting snow beneath the spruces. Proof again that "winter death has never tried the earth but it has failed." Yet, a different kind of death was succeeding. Many elms stood stark, their leaves having fallen for the last time. Some were being cut down by villagers in an effort to slow the spread of Dutch elm disease—another environmental disruption that can be laid to the hand of man. But most of the elms were showing once again that "nature's first green is gold."

The American elm has one of the most distinctive shapes among trees. Its trunk divides into branches that continue the upward thrust. Only towards the tips do the slender spray, without breaking the curve, arch toward the earth again—as if green fountains. And where the disease has not thinned their ranks, they meet above the village streets to form Gothic arches—leading toward white, straight and narrow churches, devoid of the medieval richness such trees suggest.

I read somewhere that natural enemies of imported Dutch elm disease are increasing. I hope so. We need the counterpoint of elms.

(Laconia, New Hampshire 1970)

Maine

Maine's Blackwood Campground: An afternoon fog had enveloped the rocks and now we heard thunder from behind that gray curtain. Surely, a signal. We abandoned the shore for the blue and orange tent already pitched beneath the spruces.

Tea was mentioned. Martha took the kettle and set off down the path. Wisps of fog, dull booms of thunder, the dark spruce woods—to this scene was added the loud peeping of frogs. On each side pools formed by "snow that melted only yesterday" now offered refuge to these chorusers. Fog, thunder, dark woods, white patches of snow and pools of bright water plus peeping frogs.

Then odder still, as Martha filled the kettle, a wet and ruffled Robin fluttered triumphantly from the closest pool with a small frog in his beak. This early in the spring insects were scarce, and rather than go hungry, the Robin had apparently modified his hunting techniques. Like the men of Maine, he had turned to the water. Martha was close enough to see his beak creasing the vulnerable belly of the peeper, translucent five fingered hands extending helpless on either side. Frogs are disconcertingly man-like—short fore limbs, long legs, no tail, as well as the five fingered hands and pot belly.

Hardly had the Robin flown, sparing Martha a last wave of the hands, than the remaining peepers resumed their chorus. No matter the scene, reproduction is life's most pressing business.

We talked about it for awhile over hot tea, but the storm soon drove us into the tent. And soon after that, the storm reached its climax directly over the campground. Through the fabric the lightening flashed orange and blue. Thunder muted but could not "check the peeper's silver croak." They sang out the storm and just before midnight, when the moon swam through the watery mist, they were still at it; one peeper missing, but the pool rich with spawn.

(Maine, 1970)

Arizona

Going into Arizona we were faced with more imposing officialdom than we have met at many international boundaries.

"Cars this way—Trucks that way," the signs direct. An efficient young man in a crisp uniform peered into our window.—"Any fruit or vegetables in your car?"

There were. In a webbed sack, four oranges bought in South Carolina, the last of a dozen we'd picked up in Greenville supermarket. "Let's have a look," he said.

The way he turned his face slightly off line from the oranges communicated as much as his words. "See these spots. Those are scale insects." "Insects" came out a dirty word. He extended the bag holding its tip between thumb and forefinger. "If you peel them you can bring them in."

"No," I said, defeated and not wishing to admit I would even consider eating diseased oranges. "You keep them."

He dropped the bag into some antiseptic container apparently reserved for such fruit as ours.

"And you can have these, too," I said, handing him paper towel-wrapped peels of two oranges we'd enjoyed back in liberal New Mexico.

Later we bought a few Arizona oranges to replace the Florida fruit we'd lost. Growing as they had in irrigated desert groves, they had stored less than half the juice and flavor of the others, and I did wonder then if the inspector clears out the confiscation bin and carries the contents home when no one is looking.

At least our egos fared better than they did on a crossing to California 15 years ago. We told the official we had no fruit or vegetables. He looked at our license plates and said the obvious, "You're from South Carolina. Let me look through your grocery box."

"What are you looking for?" I had asked.

"Sweet potatoes."

As though everyone from South Carolina would pack a supply of that southern delicacy across the continent just to make sure they wouldn't have to do without for even a single day.

Saturday, when we left Arizona to enter California all the man asked about was Arizona potted plants, so perhaps the Southerner's image is a touch more sophisticated. Still, next time we head west, we'll try to pack 'possum and sweet potato' and restore some sense of order to the inspectors' world.

(Arizona 1971)

Wyoming

We don't often see bears in the Tetons. Those we do observe are wild and making every effort to avoid contact with man—their dangerous, over-abundant, and unpredictable adversary. The sow with three cubs we met taught her young by example.

Driving across the sagebrush flats of Jackson Hole, Martha and I encountered this mother and her three, and in that open country they were inhospitably exposed. The distant Timbered Island with its lodge pole pines and huckleberry was far more suitable bear country and the sow raced off ahead of the car. Extended to her utmost, she reminded us of a greyhound. Between bounds, she seemed to fly over the sage with her legs stretching forward and backward in line with her body. But her cubs could not match that speed. The two larger soon fell 50 yards behind while the runt trailed miserably.

When the mother saw she could not cross to the Timbered Island ahead of us, she slowed a bit, then dashed behind us to the safety of those trees. At the edge she stopped to wait for the cubs and greeted the first two perfunctorily. Then the runt arrived all out of breath and sagged to his haunches. Though we had parked to watch, the bear didn't urge her cubs on further. She gave them plenty of time to recover from their race. But as she reassured the runt with a nuzzle, she did keep her eyes on us—made sure that we did not intend to follow her family further.

How different they were from the all but domesticated bears of many other national parks. There mother bears line their cubs along the roadsides for lessons in a combination of begging and extortion—a way of life now handed down from generation to generation, an established part of bear culture.

Those bears have forgotten the nature of humans and humans have forgotten the nature of bears. They meet in a picnic atmosphere where humans use their control over the food supply to coax an amusing performance from the bears. The bears use their superior strength and uninhibited ways to get the food as easily as possible. Fairly often, these bouts result in a hospital bill being added to the vacation expenses. A big bill was paid by a man who tried to lure a bear into the driver's seat of his car while his wife was sitting on her accustomed passenger side. He thought this would make a wonderful gag shot to show the camera club back home.

Not funny, really. Somehow, the bears must be returned to the wild ways, and the entertained visitors must come to terms with the true meaning of wilderness. The notion that we can manipulate the wilds according to our whims is both foolish and dangerous.

(Moose, Wyoming 1971)

Wyoming

None of the fish would be over five inches long. We knew that before we started our 200 mile fishing trip to southwest Wyoming—and devoted a weekend to an activity to which we are not devoted. But the tip from a visitor was too good to be ignored. We crossed the Hoback Mountains and followed the Green River towards Kemmerer.

A turn away from the river and a short side road brought us to a cut in a dry hillside and the fishing hole we sought- -a jumble of tan rock, rock easily split into thin page like layers. And within minutes, Martha had a nibble. "I found the tail of one!" she cried.

Knowing for sure that fish were there was all the encouragement we needed, and soon whole specimens were turning up in the split stone. We had discovered a school of *Knightia*, a small herring-like fish that abounded in the waters here 60 million years ago.

These fish had lived at a crucial geologic moment. Only a few hundred miles wide but reaching from the Gulf of Mexico to the Arctic Ocean, the Cretaceous Seaway was being uplifted. And the uplift continued until a shallow narrow sea became the lofty Rocky Mountains. A tropical assemblage of life forms was forced to give way to living things adapted to heights and cold.

When our school of fish died, they settled onto a muddy bottom composed of fine ash washed or blown in from nearby volcano. We found the carbon prints of land plant leaves and stems, so we assumed we were digging not far from the ancient shoreline.

No one has offered a satisfactory explanation of why these fish died and settled together on the bottom. Volcanic ash may have overwhelmed them or an algae bloom like the "red tides" along today's Gulf Coast. But one can certainly visualize similar layers of dead fish accumulating on the beds of the Great Lakes as we pour more and more DDT into our environment. Of course, the latter catastrophe applies only to our day and time.

(Kemmerer, Wyoming 1969)

The Mexican Border

A dust devil spun over the Mexican highway catching two bicyclists in a coppery maelstrom. Whipped back and forth, miraculously they kept their balance, and almost as miraculously our Volkswagen bus held the road. We might have been thrown into the desert had we not already slowed to a crawl to breast the tide of a pilgrimage.

The shoulder teemed with people. I counted a thousand in less than a mile, and along a 30-mile stretch between San Juan de Lagos and Lagos de Moreno the crowd continued to swell. Some pilgrims walked barefoot. The oldest leaned upon the young for support. Many had bound their legs with rags as though stanching wounds. All carried blankets and blackened cooking pots, equipped thus to camp in the open when night fell. And one bore, strapped to his back, a gleaming silver cross.

Later we were to discover that each Easter this pilgrimage of the poor takes place and that the destination, the chapel of San Juan de Lagos, is especially important in commemorating the Passion and Resurrection. But even on that afternoon, the cross and the fact that the following day was Good Friday, should have made it obvious that the procession was of a religious nature. Still, Martha and I had difficulty comprehending this for we had never before seen people willing to go through such effort and suffering in the name of God.

No sooner had we passed through this procession of the living, than we overcame a procession of the dead. Weeks earlier a light rain must have fallen. Not enough to wake dormant desert flowers, but where water ran off the pavement it soaked in and produced a narrow fringe of green grasses.

The fatal fringe attracted burros from miles around. Day and night they browsed—oblivious to the traffic which never slowed except after a collision. Numerous corpses sprawled on the roadside, peacefully ministered by carcasses and coyotes.

Martha remarked that the survivors wore a bemused expression. They seemed to know something ridiculous, but terribly important, that they were not about to tell.

Driving through Texas, a day to the north, we realized that only a very rich country can permit roadside vegetation to go uneaten. We came upon fields of bluebonnets and paintbrush so bright and stretching so far around that many travelers, us included, parked and strolled through the flowers, all but drowning with pleasure.

(Lagos de Moreno, Mexico 1971)

MARTHA: Early Years

As mentioned, when I was 12 I drove the car 130 miles to Grahamville from McClellanville with just my baby sister for company.

When I was 9 and Jay was 12, his father bought a house over on Scotia Street. Now he lived two whole blocks away from me. And soon after, on a Sunday afternoon, the Shuler's went for a drive—Jay, his mother and daddy and brother Boots who was nine. A pulpwood truck pulled right into them. Someone came and told his grandmother and she said, "Well, where is Bunny?" That's what they called Jay. "Jay wasn't with them," she was told. So she sent people back to the accident scene and they found Jay crawling along in the ditch. He said he didn't remember anything about the accident.

Jay's father A.T. was in the longest medical coma in the United States up until that time. He wasn't expected to live. He had lost an arm and where it was severed the medics had just tied a knot around the flesh. He had a bad cut to his head and one leg was almost off. They figured the missing arm was the least of the problems. They saved the leg. Days later when they got around to the arm they found grass and dirt was tied up inside the wound. For the rest of his life A.T. said he could feel the arm that wasn't there.

Jay's mother lived for one or two more days. His brother had been killed instantly. Jay was loved so by his mother. He was sent to the Episcopal Sunday School. He didn't know why but she wanted him to be an Episcopalian. She dressed him in a little leather jacket. This was in the Depression but she dressed both her sons so well. As an adult Jay never cared about clothes. Except for his Park Service uniform. And I polished his shoes and boots.

Jay's grandfather had given him a radio and back before the accident, we'd all go up to his room and listen. At 5:00 o'clock we'd hear creaking doors—the Shadow knew the evil that lurked in the hearts of men. Then it was "Hi ho, Silver. Away." So magical. In his room upstairs. Until the time of that wreck he was very cared for and loved. But not afterwards. He didn't get along with the woman his father married next.

Up until his mother died he was happy. I remember a Portuguese fisherman lived with them. He was a shrimper who came here as part of a fleet. The boats were little double-enders and painted blue with eyes in the bows. A.T. was out of work and this fisherman was homesick and treated Jay and Boots like his own sons. Jay's grandmother was there. She was a wonderful woman. A schoolteacher. She had taught her grown husband to read. She was always asking Jay questions. She taught him by the Socratic method. And all along he spent a lot of time over at our house and I spent a lot over at his house. His mother made the best biscuits. Syrup on top. Jay's mother was very beautiful. Jay's brother Boots could sing. He had the truest voice and played the guitar. Boots was only nine when he died. I remember him singing a song about a cowboy.

Jay at 12. Bursting out of his clothes, he seemed to grow an inch a month. By then I was following him through the woods. He let me study nature with him but I had to "get over my own fences." This was when Jay accidentally stepped on a baby rabbit and sat down and cried and I knew then what a wonderful person he was. He was like a brother. He was my playmate. We even wrote a diary together. I don't know what happened to our diary, but all my life he was my playmate.

After his father remarried, Jay went up to Orangeburg and stayed with his uncle "Buck" Shuler and Aunt Berta for two years. Berta was pregnant and had a small child also called Buck—who grew up to be a three star general. Jay stayed close to both of those boys. Just before Jay died, Buck and Jake came to see him. By then Jay couldn't recognize anybody and at first he was confused. But finally Jay smiled and said, "Buck."

But at the time of our wedding, relations with the Shuler branch were strained. A.T. had grown up in Holly Hill in South Carolina's Orangeburg County. Not exactly an aristocratic neighborhood, but A.T.'s grandfather had been a doctor up there and the grandfather was a brilliant man and pretty well known. Also A.T. had a sister who was a math professor at the University of South Carolina. Jay could have gone to Cornell and wanted to, but his father thought Clemson would make a man out of him—as the saying went. Anyway, it stands to reason that most of the Schuler's didn't think I was good enough to marry Jay. None of them came to the wedding, but Buck and Berta sent us a beautiful handmade cherry coffee table. As I said, we stayed close to that branch of the family.

The night before the wedding Mama said to me, "No one has ever called Jay ambitious. In fact, you two are the laziest people I've ever known. But, Martha, I'm sure of one thing. You'll never be bored." Mama had been watching us for our whole lives—just playing. And even now our courtship consisted of walking in the woods and planting cuttings from camellias in her yard. We didn't do anything. But it turned out that Jay wasn't all that lazy.

(Doe Hall, S.C. 2000)

JAY: Early Years

Remembering

Was it a song of triumph? Or tragedy? Is there even room in a bird brain for these "human" concepts? I think perhaps there is, but I can only tell what I saw happen. What the birds actually felt is another matter.

A pair of Carolina Wrens took the box that my father nailed under the eaves of the garage we built in our backyard. Though it happened more than 30 years ago, I remember in detail how the wrens brought leaves and straw until the box seemed ready to overflow. My brother and I put a stepladder up and with a hand mirror peeked inside. We saw four eggs. In about two weeks the eggs hatched and the parents began the busy job of keeping their offsprings fed.

Such a prosaic beginning would not have lingered so long in my memory were it not for the dramatic conclusion of the story.

From our breakfast table on the back porch we saw a blue jay fluttering in front of the birdhouse. He reached in, quickly pulled back his head and flew away with something in his beak. We checked with the mirror and could count only three nestlings.

Next morning the jay returned and repeated his robbery. Though they scolded and tried to attack the villain, the wrens were too small to deter him.

That night our father came home from a trip, and we told him what had happened. Our father saw things simply. Wrens were our friends; therefore the bluejay was our enemy. Next morning when the jay flew up, Dad was waiting with his 16-gauge shotgun.

The jay was so quick and stealthy Dad didn't have time to aim.

We were furious. The wrens were down to their last baby and we hadn't been able to do a thing to stop the thief.

Then the jay made a mistake. Until then he had limited himself to one young wren per day, but now with a scream from a nearby tree, he announced his intent to come for more. We stopped talking and froze in our positions. The jay flew straight back to the box.

Dad swung the gun up but didn't get his shot off until after the jay had pulled the last bird from the nest. Robber and nestling fell together on the driveway.

The explosion was still ringing in our ears, but the male wren did not seem to be aware there had been a shot. He flew down to his dead baby, seemed to comprehend at a glance that nothing could be done for it, then hopped atop the corpse of his enemy.

The air was filled with a new sound as over and over from his low perch he sang his clear sweet song.

(Greenville, S.C. 1969)

MARTHA: Being a Social Worker, 1945-72

Practically my first memory is of being four years old and squatting down in the dirt driveway making little circles with a stick. This shadow came over me and my neighbor Amy was standing there. She squatted down beside me and said, "I'm five years old today and Ma said I was old enough to come and see you." She lived two doors down. After that Amy Lofton and I played together every day of our young lives.

When Amy went off to college at Furman, I saw her off on the Greyhound bus and the next year I followed her. We were roommates. Of course, even knowing her, it was a shock to be off where I didn't know anybody else—to come from a village where I was loved by everyone to a campus where all the students appeared to be rich and snooty.

Plus Furman was a Baptist school and as far from home in the state as I could get—up by Greenville which even then was a city. Still, I soon made good friends and while Greenville wasn't exactly a part of the "New South" it was located halfway between Atlanta and Charlotte—and had more of a democratic spirit than Charleston and the Low Country. And being in the foothills (on a clear day within sight of the Blue Ridge Mountains) Greenville was cooler and dryer and not so overrun with that greenness, that riotous tropical growth, and the mosquitoes and horseflies I had grown up with.

My major at Furman was Sociology, and my main professor was Miss Laura Ebaugh who along with Ethel Simpson at the YWCA was among the first to fight racism in that area. Amy and I both loved Miss Laura. To protest blacks having to sit in the back of the bus, Amy and I would ride the whole bus circuit around Greenville sitting in the back. The conductors would try to get us to move forward, but we stayed put. That was in '47 or so. Miss Laura remained our close friend until her death and so did Miss Charlotte Easton.

Miss Charlotte was a tiny little woman who wore huge straw hats both out of class and in, both winter and summer. She taught botany and biology and was an excellent lecturer—teaching what she wanted and saying what she wanted in class. And she had cats. Amy and I would go to tea at her house. Cat hairs everywhere, even in the teacups. Amy shared all that with me. And aside from Jay I got my natural history education there at Furman.

After graduation I had a career as a social worker—which progressed in a trial and error fashion. I'd started out with Traveler's Aid which for the most part was incredibly boring. Two days a week I went out to the train station and sat behind a desk. I was there to serve travelers in distress but wasn't allowed to actually offer to help anyone. I couldn't initiate contact, couldn't speak first, or touch anyone, or even suggest that I might care about them in anything other than a professional way. Only one train came in per day. This was the most boringly exhausting thing I'd ever done. I finally started going into the ladies room in the afternoon and sleeping.

But the other three days a week I was at the bus station which was a busy place. I'd return run-away children and help children transfer from one bus to another. I had to get the prostitutes out of town. And I had a couple of real adventures there, too. One afternoon I was sitting at my desk and I felt somebody watching me. I looked up and this clean cut man was sort of looming over the desk. He passed me a piece of paper and said, "Will you get this to the Air Force base for me?" There was nothing on the paper but a bunch of letters and numbers. He gave me a phone number to call at the base, and then he disappeared. I didn't know what to do. My director wouldn't be any help, so I called Jay and he said dial the number and read what was on the paper to whoever answered. I did.

That night about 11 o'clock there came a pounding on our door out in Williamston. Jay and I were already asleep. Security Force investigators were there and they wanted to talk to me. Jay was cautious about letting them in. Once inside they stayed a couple of hours. Before leaving, they told me that if I saw the man again I was to follow him and call them.

So a week later (on Halloween night) the young man appeared at the desk and asked if I'd delivered the message as he asked. I said I had. I managed to keep him there a bit longer and managed to call Jay who immediately came over from Williamston—on the bus. Not surprisingly, by the time he arrived, our suspect had wandered off. But I'd followed him and finally, I looked back and with relief saw that Jay was behind me. I went back and called the OSS while Jay went on following the man in and out of bars. Instantly, it seems like, the investigators were there. They caught up with Jay and he pointed out the man.

The next day I was taken out to the base and asked to identify this mysterious character, which I did. The investigators told me that I'd never know what I had done for my country. They could never tell me. But one said if he ever could he would let me know. That was Halloween 1949 and I never heard another word. That man I'd helped to catch gave me the meanest look when I identified him—made me shiver. He looked perfectly normal until then.

Another time I confronted a crazy woman. At the bus station the people on duty were me, the janitor, a policeman, and the maid. The maid came to me saying a woman had gone crazy in the ladies room. Would I have a look? I asked the policeman to accompany me. He was just there for looks apparently. He wasn't going inside the ladies room for any reason whatsoever. So I went in by myself. This wild-haired woman had broken off a coke bottle. She chased me into one of the stalls. I locked myself in. She beat on the door threatening to kill me until the maid called the police station and they sent help.

I suppose strangest of all was my director. She had no training in social work and judged people by how "shifty" their eyes were. She instructed me to do the same.

That was Traveler's Aid. That was the job I quit to go with Jay and be a firewatcher.

When we got back from Oregon, I went to work for the Welfare Agency. This was public welfare. A lot of nice people were working there, people who were interested in their clients and would fight to the death for them. But a lot of my co-workers just had college degrees and wanted to make some money. A lot of them just plain didn't like people and certainly didn't want to be bothered by the problems of poor people. That one year I was there, I spent much of my time defending my decisions to let anyone at all receive assistance. They'd say, "Why are you putting us to all this trouble?" Then the secretary began to slip me files out of turn, saying: "I know you had the last one, but this one needs you." Otherwise these desperate people were going to be turned down. And all I was doing was going by the manual. But all that was in addition to my main job which was foster care. I had 50 children to keep in foster homes and I wanted to take everyone home with me.

That was a real burn-out job but it was the Dictaphone that did me in. We were suppose to record our interviews on the Dictaphone, but to make things as hard as possible I was usually told the machine was in use. Once the director even took it from me while I was recording. Then she did it again. Then she did it a third time. This woman was a misplaced aristocrat. Her friends had gotten her the job. She was very pretty. She wore the biggest diamond ring I had ever seen. She was very social minded—as in high society. She had no training in or interest in social work. She'd never even read the manual. That third time I put the Dictaphone on her desk. I said, "You can have it. I'm not going to work here anymore." I said, "Now, there's one thing I want to say to you. That is 'I don't think little girls from dysfunctional poverty stricken families are thinking about collecting welfare when they are in the process of getting pregnant. To collect welfare is not why they get pregnant." Awful woman.

I went to work for Amelia Croft who I knew and trusted. She was running a private United Way welfare agency—a functioning agency. I did the first interviews. Those people were scared to death. Frightened. They were humiliated. It was a terrible time for them—this asking for public assistance. Most were proud. Most had been poor all their lives so they didn't have social security. They'd never been employed at anything profitable enough to withhold from—unless it was making moonshine liquor. These people were all white. I don't think I ever had a black client to apply.

Unwed mothers. Today they're still talking about getting these women off welfare and they do have some good programs in place. The opportunities for single mothers have greatly improved since my day. Back then we just interviewed the adoptive families and the babies went. I finally had to stop seeing the unwed mothers. I knew by then that Jay and I couldn't have children and I couldn't imagine giving up a child for adoption. I started thinking the adoptive couple had to be perfect.

Finally, I just realized I was never going to resolve that issue and worked with other clients. Adolescent counseling was what I did most. I had a talent for that work. I remember one 13-year-old girl who said her stepfather was making advances. She had run away and wanted me to find a foster home for her. We had one family that would take teenagers and she stayed with them until she graduated from high school. She said to me, "I ain't lost my virginity and I don't have a beer gut. That's not how I want to live." She ended up with a very good job—much better than either Jay or I could manage. She married a good man and the last time I saw her was when she brought her little girl in to meet me. I loved that work. My boss Amelia had a masters degree in social work from Smith. She was from Eastern Maryland and what we were doing mattered so much to her. She taught me as I went. Especially about helping the children. We're still friends. Her daughter has a place down here on the coast and comes by to see me all the time.

The other good thing about Greenville was the friends we made there. We had joined the Young Democrats. My good friend Ditty Abrams drove the sound truck and Jay spoke over the megaphone telling people to vote for Adlai Stevenson. We had what we called the Tuna Club. We'd get together on Friday and make a casserole dinner. These were lawyers and doctors and their wives. They all got rich eventually— except for Jay and me. Our other friends came from a club that Jay helped to form, the Greenville Natural History Society. In the beginning the members were supposed to write papers that would be presented once a month. But they also had a once a month hike which was so successful they did it even more often. They started with ten members and when Jay left in 1972 they had hundreds—and it's still going strong. But Jay never got the scientific research club he envisioned. But he got a huge hiking club.

It wasn't just me. Everybody loved Jay.

(Doe Hall, S.C. 2000)

JAY: Being a Naturalist, 1948-72

Roan Mountain, Tennessee

A glance up Roan Mountain showed what to expect. At the crest, vapor condensing into rain caused fog to billow up and out. Still, we had come to Tennessee for the Carter County wild flower rally and refused to be shut inside.

After all, rain has compensations. Light filtered through clouds has a wonderful soft quality. Shadows dissolve and colors deepen.

We parked and took to the woods. One wishes to float on such occasions. Each heavy step crushes plants that have waited through a long cold winter to rise with the rains of spring. We could find no space for our big feet. The spongy earth was covered with violet, trillium, bellwort, and other flowers of a wonderful assortment duplicated nowhere else on earth.

A great botanist who loved these slopes claimed that if he were spun blindfolded until he lost track of time and space and then set down on this rich carpet, he could accurately name the day of the year and the particular mountain. Larkspurs were full to bursting with their throbbing blue—a blue behind which red seemed to lurk, waiting to transform the bloom at any moment.

We found a yellow lady slipper and gathered to marvel at its two-dimensional petals of twisted mahogany—a mahogany contrasted with that three-dimensional yellow lip.

Orchids! We soon located several spikes of the white and lavender showy orchids. One of our most beautiful wildflowers, they're found in almost any rich undisturbed hill or mountain woods. And unlike some orchids, they're hospitable to their would-be pollinators. These flat white lips serve as perfect landing pads for flying nectar gathers, and on this day, their lilac hoods seemed an insect's perfect shelter from the rain.

(Tennessee. 1970)

Golden Mice

We knocked, so to speak, but got no response. A half mile down the Middle Tiger River we found another Golden Mouse nest and knocked again. The second nest was empty, too. Where then, and how, do Golden Mice spend their Carolina winters?

Ambling through cane patches and groves of river birch, Martha and I were able to reconstruct a few moments in the life of a chilly muskrat. Tracks on a sandbar showed where one had gone by, his tail tracing a neat furrow among his webbed footprints. During a cold wave a few years ago, I watched a muskrat in the swamp behind the Furman University campus. He had a small hole open in the ice. Every time he dived in he broke through a skim of ice anew, but shortly he would emerge with starchy roots he had dug from the mud. He chewed them on a log, trying at the same time to extract some warmth from the pale rays that passed that day for sunshine.

But on this day no Golden Mice and no muskrats either. Not even a squirrel—but we did see where a squirrel had used a fallen tree for his table. Acorn crumbs, as yellow as egg yolks, were scattered on his tree shaped table and the mossy bank below. Either acorns were plentiful enough to waste, or the squirrel was not fond of the February menu.

At least, muskrat and squirrel had left behind a recent clue or two. Not so the mice.

In May, should one jiggle a Golden Mouse nest—a neat softball size structure felted inside with chewed bark and laced outside with cane leaves, a wide-eyed mouse will stick her head from the little side entrance. Two or more may dash out to climb nimbly among the vines and tangles where typically, they have built their home.

They use their long tails to help with climbing, not with the deftness of an opossum or monkey, but sufficiently well to steady them in precarious situations. Young Golden Mice wrap their tails around the neck of their mother when she takes them out for an excursion. Very young mice use another way to hang on.

Once, on the banks of the Seneca River near Clemson University, a tug of green briar vine brought a mother mouse scampering into the open. She had four little ones with her, each dangling from a firmly held teat. I stole away, of course, feeling slightly embarrassed and even brutish, hoping that the overloaded mother would make her way back to the shelter before any of her offspring lost its grip.

That spring day was too sweet to me. I could not bear the responsibility for the breaking of close family ties. Yet ever since, I have hoped to come on such a scene again, this time with camera handy and my heart hard enough to press for pictures.

Not today. I have camera in hand and a sufficiently hardened heart, but the Golden Mouse nests are empty. Where then, and how, do Golden Mice spend the winter?

(Greenville, S.C. 1970)

White-throated Sparrows

Tremulous, slow, in minor key, the song of the White- throated Sparrow can be heard on a sunny winter day almost anywhere. Indeed, in the Carolina Foothills they are among the most persistent singers—with a distinctive song that's been translated as, "Old Sam Peabody, Peabody, Peabody."

But Martha says it reminds her of the first line of Dvorak's *New World Symphony*, "A new cre-a-ted-world." Sad, sweet notes, and heard in early

October, we know the White-throats have returned from their summer nesting—perhaps as far as the Yukon. We tune our ears to listen and watch the feeders.

There was once a mystery about these sparrows. Ornithologists who collected and prepared the museums' long rows of eviscerated skins found unexpectedly that the bright birds with glowing yellow marks on either side of their beaks were not all males, nor were the dull birds whose yellow was reduced to a brief stain all female.

At last studies at the breeding grounds have yielded the answer. There are two color phases of White-throated Sparrows, the bright phase containing twice as many males as females. And the dull phase where the females outnumber males two to one.

Then came a startling discovery. A difference in behavior accompanies the plumage changes.

The bright males are more aggressive, tend to sing more often and more strongly and in clashes with their dull brothers almost always have their way. The bright females are not only bolder than their dull sisters; on occasion they burst into unladylike song.

Obviously, courtship is complicated under these circumstances. Out of 213 pairs examined, 136 pairs were bright males mated to dull females; 70 dull males were mated to bright females; six pairs were recorded as both dull and only one pair out of the whole sample of 213 consisted of two bright birds. Theirs must have been a stormy relationship.

(Greenville, S.C. 1969)

Gap Creek

We went to say good-bye to Gap Creek. We parked our cars, a dozen or more, a mile beyond Rudy's Grocery, there where the pavement ends.

Where the pavement ends! Will it ever? For it is another extension of pavement that has brought about the massacre of as beautiful a community of Appalachian plants and animals as could be found in South Carolina—or the nation.

Last spring I went alone to Gap Creek to see if the Adder's-tongue Fern was out yet. It was. Beds of large flowered trillium were blooming, too—Gap Creek's unique variety with streaks of green running through the white petals and aging to pink flecked with crimson. So was Vasey's trillium, yellow mandarin, and marsh violet. And there among them I saw the mark of doom, a surveyor's stake driven into the rich woods soil. Forgetting the flowers, I followed the stakes. They led through the heart of the valley. They were clearly the first on-site step of building a road. In our foolish, short sighted society we always destroy the streams and their valley's first. We seal up with artificial rock the most precious natural resource we have, land where things can grow.

Few places on Earth have been undisturbed for so many ages as our foothills and mountains. Through millions of years the forest community has been refined, enriched, integrated, until it is a true wonder of this world.

More salamanders exist here than anywhere else. (I wonder if every Clemson Salamander will die as the dams are built at Jocassee?) More trilliums, too. And a number of relict plants whose closest relatives are found in the woods of China and Japan.

As we started up the dirt road there were few signs of what was to come. True, couches, old stoves, and other discarded paraphernalia were in evidence. The Tar Heels have been dumping these across the state line for years. I do not take joy in that, but I don't grieve over the matter either. Leaves falling as steadily as years slip by will cover the junk over. Knowing what we would soon find, the sofas in the forest seemed benign, almost poetic.

Around the next bend came the jolt. We had tried to prepare ourselves for loss, but one never can. The relentless bulldozers had swept over the ridge and down to the stream destroying everything on their appointed route—cutting deep into the flesh of the mountain. And these wounds will not soon heal; they will fester with landslides—though the engineers may claim to have worked all that out.

Too many of these rare places have died in the last few years. Once crucified, no river valley ever rises from the dead.

Goodbye, Gap Creek.

(Greenville, S.C. 197O)

Mushrooms

"Look for them when oak leaves are at the mouse-ear stage," admonishes the author of one mushroom book. Yet when friend Myra Davis showed me morels volunteering in her garden, azaleas and dogwoods were bursting into bloom—and her oaks, I judged to be a little past the mouse-ear stage. From my somewhat specialized viewpoint, the morels were by far the most exciting plant before us. Over two dozen of the fruiting bodies were up, brown like the litter of the forest floor, and tending even here to blend into the background.

It takes a keen and educated eye to find them. Two summers ago Myra shared a batch with Martha and me in the Tetons, so she knew what to look for. Last season in Wyoming was even better. Martha, who has an uncanny knack for finding things, whether papers I have lost, arrowheads in the fields or morels in the woods, probably harvested over 500 of them.

Of all the edible mushrooms, morels are the most sought after by mycophagists (mushroom eaters). The flavor is rich and yet they have few calories—until they're simmered in butter and resting in a thick cream—by which time calories are beside the point.

I am tempted to say that their form is so unusual they cannot possibly be confused with other mushrooms. But the caution bell rings when I consider that any child on our street can identify an automobile make from a hundred yards while I have to get close enough to read the name printed on the trunk.

Wrongly identifying a poisonous mushroom has far more serious consequences than guessing Ford for Chevrolet.

Be warned. But don't be counting on a domesticated version any time soon.

Much research and effort has gone into the cultivating of morels, but with limited success. The mycelium, white threads that are the underground part of the plant can be grown, but no fruiting bodies are produced. A fortune awaits the person who solves that problem.

Still, they shouldn't count on Martha and me to be customers. The purchased flesh may be sweet, but the spirit of a tramp through the woods, the exhilaration of spring, the charm of a gift from nature, would all be missing from such an enterprise. Or maybe we could just have lunch in Myra's garden.

(Greenville, S.C. 1969)

MARTHA: Photography. 1952-94

Coming back from our summer of fire watching in Oregon, Jay got a job as a counter man in an electrical supply store. Our friend Wesley Davis got him that job. Wesley was a self made man, an electrical engineer—and by then he was doing very well. He had such broad interests and fortunately one of those interests was our welfare.

The other thing we'd done was to buy a small house. The neighborhood was on the edge of Greenville but within the city limits. It even bordered on a small city park. The house was well built with hardwood floors and a basement. But tiny. Four rooms. They called it five but that last room was just an arched over breakfast nook. But the lot was large and wooded and we didn't have to pay but $7500. In the beginning we only had one set of neighbors. A football coach and his wife. We all got along great. Eventually, other houses were built and they were all larger and more expensive.

By then we were both working at full time jobs, but Jay had become more and more interested in nature photography. His interest grew while we were in Oregon, and he bought a 35 mm Nikon Camera that he would use for the next 20 years. He realized that his slides, as beautiful as they were, needed a practical application in order to sell. We decided that nature study instruction for the schools was the answer. We started out making the slides ourselves. Wesley Davis had a small stainless steel box built. This would hold 16 rolls of film that we could submerge in the bathtub which held the chemicals. Using a thermometer, I'd mix up the developing formula in the kitchen. Jay could never get this exactly right. The bathroom was the darkroom—sealed off from light from both door and window. We submerged the films, hung them to dry and then clipped off each individual image and ironed it on the ironing board. Then we packaged them in little wooden boxes and included a printed text which Jay had written. We pasted a pretty label on top and were in business. Sort of.

Doing all this usually took until 2:00 in the morning. I was working during the day and Jay was too. Eight hours of that and eight hours on photography naturally led to sleep deprivation. One night we ran out of hanging space on the lines and Jay propped a mop handle across a door frame. The mop fell down. Jay just tossed everything back in the bath and the slides came out fine. But sooner or later we were going to need some sleep.

Fortunately, Wesley Davis took an interest at this point. He enjoyed bird watching and was intrigued by Jay's perceptions. Jay had already won many nature photography awards by then. Wesley said, "Jay, quit the job as a counterman, go full time into your photography business, and I'll send you a check for $100 every week for a year." Well, they wanted to promote Jay where he was and send him on the road as a salesman. Jay said, "I'll take it on the condition I can pay you back when I'm able." Wesley agreed but when Jay was finally able to pay him, Wesley told him to give the money to Clemson which they had both attended—and insisted that Jay give the $5200 in his own name. Which the University never quite understood since Jay had never given a penny before or after that donation. Nevertheless, Clemson did eventually name him a "distinguished graduate." Wesley Davis asked us not to speak of his generosity—which had made all this possible—and we didn't. He never told a soul. Years later he did tell his wife Myra. That was the kind of man he was. Such a good friend. Such a good man.

So with Wesley's aid we succeeded with the filmstrip business. Eventually we found a company that could do all the development work just as cheaply as we could do it ourselves. We had a team of salesmen working—Jay's uncle, Dick Bob Morrison, and the girl from across the street and Jay, himself. The slides weren't hard to sell because the teachers loved them.

And eventually we made money—enough to build a tremendous beautiful house down on the coast near McClellanville.

Then once back in the low country, we sold out our company to Carolina Biological, a school supply company in North Carolina. Jay kept photographing for them but gradually filmstrips were being replaced with video. The teachers all told us they preferred Jay's strips to the video because they could halt the machine—freeze the image—and lecture. But video replaced them anyway. We were rich but only for a while—that was in the mid 1960's.

Back in 1956 we had a tragedy in the family. My older brother Sonny's wife Kitty died in childbirth. And she and Sonny had had a child killed by a car the previous year. All this loss was too much for my brother. We went to the funeral and my uncle, a judge in nearby Georgetown, said to me, "Everybody thinks that you and Jay should take care of the children. Sonny's in no shape to do it." I said we would think about it. I told Jay and he said, "Why, of course. I was thinking the same thing just this morning."

Jay and I weren't able to have children. While he was a young man he'd gone into an infirmary with a case of poison ivy that practically covered his body. And someone there had treated his scrotum with x-rays—which they now know kills your sperm forever. Not understanding what had happened, we'd kept going around to fertility experts for years. So sad. I told him I didn't care, that I didn't marry him to have children.

But as it turned out we had somebody living with us most of our married life, anyway. Money was tight and someone's child, college age or younger was always sleeping on the couch. My sister Emily was at Furman. Daddy had a couple of bad jobs and didn't have the money for her room and board. She slept on the couch. Then her old roommate came, as well. The roommate had been dating our cousin and her parents didn't approve of him. They cut off her college funds. She got a job to pay her tuition and slept in our living room until the day she graduated—which was also the day she married our cousin. Emily began to date Oran Baldwin who we call Zero. He'd drive over from Clemson. He had an old Crosley automobile that he'd lean up against a tree and work on all weekend. Their courtship consisted of Emily handing him tools—as opposed to mine which was following Jay through the woods. They got married in July of 1952.

A few years later we took in one of Tunk and Ev's children. Ev was my aunt, married to my mother's brother, but close to our age. Malcolm, one of her middle children, was failing in school. He was nine. All he did was read comic books. They knew he was bright. So we took him in— gave him the couch in the living room. We cut off the TV and gathered up the comic books. He began to study and turned into an A plus student. He stayed one year and a summer in the Tetons. And eventually he got scholarships to Furman and medical school. He's a commander in the navy. He and his wife have six children.

But we had Sonny's children for the longest time. We actually adopted Harrington when he was nine. That was a choice we gave both children. Sara went home to Sonny after four years. She was fourteen.

Just the other day I was laughing with Sara over her ice rink skirt. We tried to keep the children busy with after school activities. Sara got very good at figure skating, but all the other girls had fancy skirts, elaborate costumes to skate in. We had no money so Jay made Sara's skirt. He laid out a piece of blue felt, cut it in a circle, and attached a snap at the waist. And then since he couldn't actually sew, he glued on the decoration of a white fish complete with rising bubbles. Sara was the envy of every girl.

Jay did so much with those children. He took them on photographing expeditions to Pisgah Forest in North Carolina and very often to the nearby Furman campus. He taught them the names of every plant and animal around. He read to them. I can still remember his "Winnie the Pooh." He did every voice different and was especially adapt at Eeyore—the sighing, gloomy donkey.

Jay made a difference in their lives and I believe I did, as well. Still, I must admit, that after four years of parenting I was on the verge of a nervous breakdown. I was trying to be the perfect mother, perfect choir director, perfect den mother, and work full time. And though we had had people coming and going over the years, this sudden and continuing responsibility was overwhelming. Plus I was grieving for my sister-in-law. Fortunately, I ended up with a wonderful psychiatrist who convinced me pretty quickly that I couldn't be all things to all people. A good doctor and a good friend—he's brought his family down to camp here. I still chat with him on the phone.

In the early 70's Harrington was enrolled at the University of Georgia, but he wasn't happy and quit to go shrimping like his daddy, Sonny. Sonny had married a wonderfully outspoken woman, Hazel, who set his life in the right direction. Sonny had been doing well shrimping. Then he designed and built a tremendous steel hull boat and did even better. So Harrington moved back to McClellanville and with a little help from Sonny, built a similar boat, which, of course, is amazing in itself. And Harrington shrimped for years and made money. He's married now to Caroline, who is Cilla's niece. They live in Fernandia, Florida, and have two children. And Sonny's daughter Sara has two children. A boy who has given her two grandchildren and a daughter in Atlanta who has one of those amazing careers young people have—with computers.

But to get back to the ancient 1960's and 70's. Jay and I had a Volkswagen camper and even amongst the coming and going of children and boarders, we kept traveling—we kept looking at the natural world—all that beauty. We just kept going along with Jay being the scout and calling out "Mart, look at this!"

(Doe Hall, S.C. 2001)

JAY: Florida, 1970

Oranges

The heavily laden bee struggled to gain altitude. Then smashed into our windshield. A large drop of colorless orange-blossom nectar ran down the glass.

We had entered the soft tropical air of Florida an hour or so earlier. The boundary was sharp. One moment we were driving through a cold Georgia rain and the next our car windows misted over like a glass of iced tea set out on a hot summer day.

Except for the cities and tourist spots, peninsular Florida is a vast orange grove. The vegetation imposed on the landscape by man is symmetrical—both in rows set out and the repeated shape of the individual plants. Orange trees are as globular as the fruit hanging from their branches, and in mass, they plaid the rolling hills—patched here and there by the disk-shaped lakes that are formed by collapsing limestone cavities.

Tiny white buildings, higher than wide, stand close beside these lakes and are reflected in the water. These are honeybee cities, haphazardly stacked hives where hard work is done. While orange trees bloom, 10,000 bees in each box labor to exhaustion, fanning the nectar with their wings to reduce sweet liquid to sweeter honey.

We stopped to buy some oranges (the trees bear flowers and ripe fruit at the same time) and a breeze blowing from the groves seemed heavy enough to distill for honey. And that heady atmosphere extended to the campground where we repaired for the night.

Orange-blossom breezes wafted even through the restroom. On the lavatories and mirrors translucent green tree frogs plied their profession which is the capture of insects attracted to lights. If the frogs were jade then their eyes were jet, animated gems that followed every move of their prey.

I wet a finger and let a single drop of water fall on one of the frogs. He drew up as though waiting with pleasure to receive the next. Every second they are out of the water, frogs, and all other amphibians, are threatened with death by drying.

On the walk back to our tent, I caught sight of the moon. All solar eclipses occur on a day when the moon is new, so with an eclipse exactly two weeks behind us, this one was (as it should be) full. A full moon framed through a twisted moss-hung oak. Oak, moon, and moss softened and diffused by moisture laden perfumed air.

(Everglades, Fla. 1970)

MARTHA: Doe Hall 2001 and Florida, 1970

I called Walt Rhodes, the wildlife man, about our out-of-control alligators, and he immediately put me on the defensive by saying that the city of Mt. Pleasant had concreted over all the alligator habitat. That was a bit of an exaggeration. Mt. Pleasant is the community just north of Charleston and south of us. It's bursting at the seams and threatening to move this way—but I wouldn't say that was all the alligator habitat in the world.

But he went on claiming that the alligators had no place left to go and did I want them to become extinct. And I said, "No, Walt. You know me better than that. And you knew Jay's feeling on those matters." He said, "That's right. Think of what a naturalist Jay was. How can you even think of getting rid of an alligator?" I said, "It's true Jay wouldn't be making this call or approve of me making it, but he's dead. And I have to make these decisions now. My grandchildren are running around here, and my friends want to bring their dogs and can't. He said, "Martha, if I picked them all up today, you'd have another there tomorrow. All you can do is fill in your pond with dirt."

"Completely?" I asked. "Walt, is that what you want me to do?" The pond is at least 20 acres—but I suppose he thinks that's within the capabilities of my brother Horry's construction business. He shouts, "No! Of course not!" I said, "Alright. Let's get rid of the biggest. You know, last winter just as soon as you told me on the phone that alligators don't eat in the winter, I looked out my bedroom window, and 50 yards away the biggest one in the pond was up on the bank eating something that looked like a whole pig. Whatever he caught had black fur and was bloody inside. That was January,

Walt, and whether you know it or not this is a sub tropical climate, and our alligators like those in the Everglades are always on view. I love them Walt. I have nothing against reptiles. But I don't want a ten-foot alligator dozing under my window or stalking the dog and me when we go out. How about take the big ones?"

By then we'd talked a half hour on my dime and he came around to the point of saying that he couldn't just take out the big ones, but he would get some bounty hunters to do it. If I would point out the culprits that would help. But, of course, in the eyes of the naturalists I was going to look pretty bad.

I thanked him. And eventually the larger ones were removed.

What had started this off was an alligator lunging up the bank at Emily and Zero's grandchild. The boy was crabbing. Plus Zero had four toddlers out there. Those darlings are just alligator size and the joy of this place is to have the children play here. I swear that alligator was 15 feet. Alright. 12 feet!

Last month they were making their love songs. They bellow. My little dog Wolfie sat up and listened—ears perked straight up. Then a great horned owl started in. That did it for Wolfie and he jumped into my lap.

I've actually held alligators in my hand while they're hatching out. They make a cute chirping noise. Their little snouts poke out of the egg. Jay said, "Watch out. They're already big enough to bite the tip of your finger off." He was making a recording of the sounds. The mother was watching us. We were careful to put the babies back as we found them. Fifteen or so. The mother stayed right there watching us. She was big enough to bite off an arm or leg.

The last nest I found here, my nephew Michael ran over with the bush hog. Jay would never have stood for that either. He wouldn't let them even kill a poisonous snake—no snakes at all, venomous or otherwise. A few years before he died, I saw him in the yard with a snake wrapped around the end of a rake—Jay on one end and snake on the other. He was moving it off into the woods. He came in the house and said, "That was the prettiest canebrake rattler I've ever seen." He couldn't possibly have killed him. He added, "I haven't seen very many, though." I said, "And I hope you don't see many more."

I killed a copperhead last year to protect the dog. I figure I've got a right to be here too. But all this talk of alligators and snakes brings me around at last to the Everglades. Back in the early 60's Jay and I started going there each Christmas. Harrington would return to McClellanville to hunt ducks with his daddy, but I was involved with foster care, so we still couldn't leave until Christmas day. We'd stay six or seven days. I believe the best Christmas dinner I ever had was down there. We were camping with two friends and had reservations at a nice restaurant in Homestead. Peking Duck was their special for Christmas. We four were sitting around in lounge chairs waiting to go. Then we put together cheese, bread and butter and a bottle of wine. We never went to the restaurant. We sat and talked. We took a walk. Then we sat and talked until the stars came out. Then we crawled into our tents and went to sleep.

Another of those Florida Christmases Jay gave me my diamond ring. We'd been married forever. The morning we were leaving for Florida he tossed it in my lap and teased me with, "You like little things." A beautiful one carat brilliant diamond ring. I couldn't believe my eyes. Each morning in the tent the first thing I'd do was stick out my hand and admire it.

Tents are the most wonderful shelters. They're great for marriages. You're thrown together—very closely thrown together. Tents are very cozy little places. All the world is around on the outside, but inside were just me and Jay. Tents are very sexy.

So down in Florida and a lot of other places, that fold of canvas was our own little home. And sometimes we skipped the tent. If we knew it wasn't going to rain we just threw the sleeping bags on the ground. Whatever we did, we were always disdainful of those streamlined coaches. That wasn't camping to us. We might as well have taken our house along.

I already mentioned that Jay and I camped in every state except Hawaii and Alaska—we ran out of time before we got to them. We met such wonderful people in campgrounds. Of course, our camping ended 20 years ago, and I suppose they have more crime, more crowding since. But for us those campgrounds were safe and usually empty places. We particularly loved the primitive Forest Service camping areas. They'd have an outdoor toilet and a hand pump. That was all. I've had some wonderful baths under those hand pumps—just ponderosa pines for a shower curtain. A friend told me that in Africa during WWII she used to bathe in a helmet of water. That was all that was allowed. I've had that kind many a time. But the bath that really stands out in my mind was taken down in the Florida Everglades. Jay and I broke into a maintenance shed and got into the giant tub they used to clean mops. We stood in there and took turns throwing buckets of water on each other. Oh, to be clean. You just can't explain how good that feels.

(Doe Hall, S.C. 2001)

JAY: Florida, 1970

Passion

We entered the garden through a gate twined with crimson and purple passionflowers—and paused enthralled.

The tropical Eden confronting us was actually Redland Fruit and Spice Park, a broad collection of ornamental and useful plants set out by the Dade County Parks and Recreation Department in 1944. No easy task, for the workmen had to dig with picks into Miami oolite, a hard limestone laid down in a shallow sea some 100,000 years ago.

Our own chore was more pleasurable, for we had come to find the Spot-breasted Oriole, a Central American bird, which in some unexplained way has established in Florida. Martha soon sighted one in a loquat grove. A lovely bird, he was as bright as the Baltimore Oriole, but with a curious patch of spots on either side of his breast.

This newcomer promises to take over as one of the most common as well as most colorful birds in the area. But with so much fruit to eat, many birds have been attracted to the 20-acre park. We saw several warblers. On the spring journey north, this was perhaps their first rest stop in the states. And one, just tantalizingly glimpsed, might have been the rare Kirtlands Warbler. It worked into the depths of a Spiny Ancoba tree and was lost from sight. But nearby, a pair of more mundane sparrows flitted to the top of a Surinam Cherry—a broad tree heavy with red fruit.

Many cherries had fallen on the ground, and Martha picked up one and sniffed it. And as she did so, she recited from the big sign on the passionflower gate. We were not to eat the park's fruit. She handed a cherry to me and I ran my fingers over the fleshy ridges that radiated from stem to navel. A decidedly exotic appearance.

"Wonder what it tastes like?" sighed Martha.

"Why don't you go ahead and eat one," said our friend from Anderson—whose accent goes faintly sibilant on occasion. "Surely the rule doesn't apply to nibbling a little cherry picked up off the ground."

"Mmmmmmm, delicious," Martha said as she tasted hers and passed one on to each of us.

Then a deep voice in the distance called out, "Come to the gate." The command sounded oddly impersonal, yet compelling, and we blanched guiltily.

I glanced at my watch. This Garden of Eden was not scheduled to close until 4:30 and it was barely past the hour. But the command was repeated louder and with even more force. Slowly we walked over to the gate to face the consequences.

"You'll have to leave," he said.

"But we thought the park stayed open til 4:30."

"Usually it does. But my ride home is waiting and I'll have to walk if I miss it."

He swung the gate shut behind us and snapped the lock— which caused the passion flowers to tremble.

(Homestead, Fla. 1970)

MARTHA: Show Business, 1960's

Beginning in 1962, Jay began to work for the U.S. Park Service in the summers. First we were in the Blue Ridge Mountains and then spent six years in Wyoming's Grand Tetons. Jay loved that work. Besides being an excellent naturalist, he understood how to present what he knew. He had a good voice and whether leading a hike or hosting a slide lecture at night, he enjoyed an audience. He could project his voice. His manner was so quiet, it often surprised people when he got behind a podium. Especially if he was fighting to preserve some portion of the wilderness.

Back in Greenville, Jay had once been scheduled to appear in a play opposite Jo Ann Woodward (Paul Newman's wife) but in the end they decided he was too tall—or maybe he couldn't act well enough. But he'd thought about acting professionally. And actually, Jay did have a television career which I might as well mention here—though I'm not sure when this was—the 60's maybe.

Jay did a series of programs called "Spying on Nature" for the public television station. This was broadcast from Columbia which is in the middle of South Carolina. And the complications of Jay making that drive is all I really remember about the whole program.

You see, they told Jay he had to have a toupee because the television lights shone off of his baldhead. But he couldn't get this hairpiece on straight and had to go to my hairdresser to have it set. Then, since he had to drive to Columbia with the window down, she had to start covering the toupee up with a hair net. I remember our neighbor's child, Michie, coming up to Jay as he was getting in the car. Michie went, "Jay?" Jay says, "Michie." Michie says, "Is that you?" "Yes, it's me." "Did you get a hair cut or something?"

Somewhere I have photos of Jay in his toupee in front of the camera, his hands on a giant rattler. He has the fangs forced over the edge of an old time sundae glass and he's "milking" out the venom.

(Doe Hall, S.C. 2001)

Poetry 1948 and Much Later

Jay's Aunt Ev had married my Uncle Tunks and they lived off down in Grahamville. And both being the youngest in their families, they were only ten years or so older than Jay and I, and we were close friends. Anyway, for our wedding, Tunks stayed home to take care of their two-week-old baby girl, Linky, and Ev brought the more elderly Horry women to McClellanville for the festivities.

The wedding: And the honeymoon: Jay woke me up that morning. Mama was trying to keep him out of my room—since it was bad luck to see the bride before the ceremony. But he said, "Good gracious, Miss Mary (he didn't start calling her 'mother-in-law' until after the service and for the rest of their life together) Miss Mary, we have work to do." Then he kissed me on the forehead and said, "Get up girl." "Why?" I asked. He said, "We have to help your uncle Heyward fix the flowers." Which we did. All the flowers were wild—bouquets and corsages. The yellow fringe orchids were blooming. Jay and I helped with those up until time for the bride's maid luncheon-which I went off to with my hair still up in curlers.

I mean I knew absolutely nothing about protocol, had no social graces. The luncheon was a very formal affair and I walked in with my hair in curlers and was so embarrassed. All I can say is the family always thought I was a bit eccentric and let me go that way—accepted me that way. Then the priest married us and we had the wedding reception at my home. Emily had painted the front of the house herself just for the reception and we made all this food. Jay and I smiled at everyone until our jaws ached.

Finally it was time for us to drive away on our honeymoon. Well, Jay couldn't drive, but he insisted on at least being behind the wheel when we left, and then down the road towards Charleston I took over. We got across the Cooper River Bridge and to the far side of Charleston, and stopped for supper. Afterwards the car wouldn't start. Jay pushed and it started. As a joke the groomsmen had pulled a wire loose, assuming that Jay would spot that easily and fix it. We didn't know that. Jay didn't know how to drive much less look underneath the hood. But we were on the road again.

We got down to Grahamville. The Horry family had lent us a cabin on the Broad River for the honeymoon. I knew the way there—except that a detour sign was up. I took this strange road that led way out into the river marshes. We came to a seemingly impassable little wooden bridge and Jay got out to check that. He waved me on. But the car cut off. And wouldn't start. Jay started pushing on the fender.

This was the middle of the night and I was exhausted. I steered the car straight into a rice field. It sank to the axles in the mud. And Jay had disappeared from sight.

I thought, "My God, I've killed my husband and I've only just gotten him." But in a moment he came slogging and sputtering out of the mud to stand in the headlights. "Goddamn!" he shouted, "This is the only suit I've ever owned." (Actually, he didn't own many more in the years to come.)

We knew we'd have to walk back to the paved highway for help. We had the moonlight. I could see my white satin slip shining. My going-away dress was in the most modern 1948 style, with skirt tapering down tight around my ankles. Naturally, I couldn't walk in that, so I hiked the material up and tied it off with Jay's belt. My sister-in-law Kitty had made all my underwear. Satin underwear including that slip that was shining in the moonlight. We went walking along the road with the rut between us but holding hands. Jay was worrying about rattlesnakes but I was too exhausted to even care—until a horse neighed. I jumped over the rut into Jay's arms. "Mart," he said, "that's just a horse."

Finally, we saw lights down the road and came to a black cabin. Cars in the yard. A woman came to the door. All the men were off playing poker and had left no car keys. We asked how far to the highway? "Ain't too far," came the answer. Then a pause. "But it's a good piece if you walking."

We kept walking and reached the highway as dawn was breaking. A milk truck was the first vehicle to come by and bless his heart, the milkman stopped. He had one crate I could sit on and Jay who was too tall to stand in the truck, knelt beside me and held on. The driver knew exactly where Tunks and Ev lived. He was carrying milk there.

So we reached Grahamville, went inside, and woke Tunks up. Ev was still back in McClellanville. Tunks told us to crawl into his bed and he'd go over to sleep at his mother's. He said, "There's a bottle in the refrigerator if the baby wakes up." That was the two-week-old Linky he was keeping. Poor baby. If she cried I didn't know it. I passed out in my muddy white satin slip and the next thing I knew it was mid morning. Tunks was back in the kitchen giving the baby a bottle and the car was sitting in the front yard. Tunks who was a master mechanic and master rigger had already gotten it out of the mud, fixed the wire and washed it off, and we had no more car problems. That was the honeymoon.

Which does bring me in a very round about way to poetry.

I was reading over Jay's poetry last night. It made me so sad. Back in the early 60's when most of it was written, I had other things to worry about—trying to care for Sonny's children and dealing with all that associated loss. But I can see now that Jay was troubled—so much of his poetry written about death—confidences shared on parting.

His Aunt Ev Horry kept up his interest in poetry. Both were members of the Georgia Poetry Society. They published a book of poetry together. They split the book, with Jay providing "A Confidence" and Ev "On Parting" to the title. It sold pretty well for poetry—though selling poetry isn't the point.

And Ev and Tunks stayed close to us—in our hearts. Ev would drive those 130 miles from Grahamville on the spur of the moment. Tunks was a well driller by profession, but like my brother-in-law, Oran, he could patch together amazing mechanical inventions. He put the elevator in this house I'm in. He got the pieces off a junk pile or out of a surplus catalogue—and it goes up and down just fine.

But the tragedy in their lives, in all our lives, was losing Linky. That little baby Tunks was holding back in 1948 grew up to be a beautiful and gentle woman. She married a young man in McClellanville and they had two children. She became a postal clerk. A man came into the post office and murdered her. A completely senseless loss.

Below is one Jay's poems, one that deals with loving nature, and a second on "Small Love" will be coming along in the next chapter.

QUIETNESS

Quietness comes
Bringing the little noises
Now we can smell the pine
And hear the fragile wind
We did not know was there
When we stood across the dunes
Listening to surf.

There is the kinglet.
And hear! The breeze again.

From: A Confidence on Parting

Mexico, 1961

I had heard there was a mission down in Mexico, one popular with birders, where you could stay cheap. So in the spring of 1961, we got our usual $300 ahead in life and said, "Let's go." We got Harrington out of school. Naturally, with so little money we had to camp which we wanted to do anyway. But I did ask Jay to buy us a real folding toilet seat. This cost $8 or $10—just a seat that went over a hole in the ground. But Jay insisted on saving money by making me one out of a camper stool. The very first night I set it up behind a pine bush. The stool collapsed and a loose wire put a big gash on my leg. I was furious. "You couldn't spend $8 on me!" But he fixed it.

We had a beautiful trip all the way down. Gorgeous country in Mexico. I spotted a sign saying Queratoro and I'd read that the best topaz cutters in all of Mexico were there. We turned off. Had lunch in the little town and asked at the restaurant who the best cutters around were. We were sent down the street to a tiny shop where a man had just finished setting this beautiful topaz into a ring which he said was gold. He had hammered the gold setting.

Well, I like jewelry. To this day, I do. Immediately, I fell in love with that ring. My sin—my terrible failing, this weakness for jewelry. The man wanted $19. That was $19 out of our $300, which had to last us three months. Jay said, "Mart, it's just brass and glass and we can't afford it anyway." So we were going up the mountain. And I was thinking about the ring. Tears were running down my cheeks. And Jay saw that. He turned the Volkswagen around, went back and bought the ring.

The next year when we went back to the Blue Ridge Parkway, one of the Park Service gemologists said, "That stone is beautiful. Where'd you get it?" "Mexico." I took the ring off and handed it to him. Jay said, "Just brass and glass." But the gemologist wanted to test it, and we agreed. He took the ring in the back room and when he came back out, he said, "I don't know what you paid for it, but I'll give you $2200." I was so happy. I said, "No.

This is my ring." And I still have that topaz ring. That ring is the only thing in our marriage that I cried for and got. "A perfect champagne topaz," the gemologist said.

That was Mexico. A place of many surprises. But I have to back up. I had my ring and we headed on to the mission. We arrived there in the dark—rainy. And this gray-haired man ran out into the rain with his arms outstretched. "Welcome children!" he shouted. We didn't make reservations. Nobody did. They didn't know we were coming but still we were welcome. Welcome despite the fact that the mission was full and not one spare bed was available. We were put up in the attic in a curtained off space. The maid also had a curtained space and Harrington had another. The bathroom was downstairs.

The rafters of the attic were hung with bunches of bananas—hands of bananas—and at night the vampire bats would come in and roost on the hands of bananas. That first night I said, "Jay?" He said, "Don't worry. They're not the least bit interested in you. They're roosting." And they never did bother us. At night the bananas were black with roosting bats. Harrington believed everything Jay said, so he was happy. The windows were open and the bats would fly in and out. The other demand made on us—beside the bats—was the church service we were expected to attend every morning at 6:00. The service was in Spanish. The hymns in Spanish. This was a Seventh Day Adventist mission. We didn't mind. We needed to be up that early to photograph and would set out as soon as the service ended. Oh, Jay was in heaven. He really did see beauty everywhere especially down there. He'd be saying, "Mart, look at this! Mart, look at this!" Through the entire day.

One of Jay's prime interests was the Guatemalan Royal bird. We wanted to pay the village boys to find the nest and then we could set up the camera and flash at these sites. But no one quite understood our purpose and assumed we wanted to smuggle out the bird pelts which was apparently a big business. They'd rub the skins down with oatmeal as a preservative and sell them to smugglers—who hid the skins in the tire wells of cars. They were scrupulously honest about our possessions but not about the birds. They kept bringing us dead ones. Jay would say, "No! No!" or the Spanish equivalent and finally one boy understood and began to show us the nests.

Life in the mission was perfect. We ate what the Seventh Day Adventists ate. They were vegetarians. We'd buy milk and cheese when we went into the town and cook them soufflés and macaroni and cheese dishes. They couldn't cook at all on their Sabbath which was Saturday. We asked if we could cook for them on that day which they loved. They were the sweetest people. So innocent. Unfortunately, the doctors knew very little about medicine—even though they were trained in California. But the local people came in because the doctors were so kind and occasionally they would hit on a cure and help someone.

They helped Jay when he broke his leg. He climbed a tree to photograph an orchid and coming down, a limb snapped off and fell and Jay fell with it. He broke his ankle. And even worse, I was parked a half mile away and he had to limp through poison ivy to get to me. I drove him back to the mission and they were thrilled, because somebody had just given them a new x-ray machine and they could practice on Jay. Then they put a cast on his leg which was terrible because the poison ivy began to itch beneath the cast. And Jay could only scratch it by sliding a ruler under the cast.

They did move us from the attic to an upstairs bedroom. And they gave Jay dozens of Seventh Day Adventist books to read—certain that with a captive audience they could convert him. They'd come in and talk about the books which Jay did read, but they hadn't actually read them, so Jay knew more about their religion than they did. Still, they were very sweet and very kind to us both, and today their medical school in California is much improved and especially well known for its treatment of children's diseases.

Well, we left not too long after Jay's accident. I was going to drive, but Jay said that wasn't necessary. And soon after the cast did come off. In order to relieve the itching of the poison ivy, one day Jay went swimming in the Pacific and the cast just dissolved. (The plaster of Paris and all the other medical supplies were sent down to Mexico because their shelf life was long over.) Anyway, Jay just hopped around until we could get back to Greenville. His orthopedist said he'd never seen x-rays as beautiful as those taken at the mission. He said, "For God's sake stay out of trees. This is your second break on that ankle." And he put on a walking cast and Jay was fine and went right on climbing trees to get photographs—or lying down on the roadside to get those tiny little flowers. Years later when he was doing a series on fiddler crabs, I remember him just lying down in the mud with the mosquitoes covering his back. And he went right on photographing.

But to get back to Mexico. I have a few pages of a log I kept—obvious pre-falling out of the tree days. This is for May 27, 1961:

> *My 34th birthday. I feel younger and healthier than I can ever remember! Marie sang "happy birthday", Sigrid picked a bouquet and gave me a Dutch chocolate bar, Harrington did the breakfast dishes (we do them on the "Sabbath") and Jay was especially sweet and thoughtful, so birthdays at remote missions in Mexico are just as festive and special as anywhere else! This being rest day, we went to Tata Santa. Harrington swam, Jay birded and I donned my bathing suit and read in the sun on a beach towel. We had a lovely soup (Lipton's chicken and canned bouillon mixed) and a dessert of bread with a topping of peanut butter, bananas and orange marmalade. We spent a couple of hours strolling through our orchid woods where I picked a bouquet (a four foot spray) of orchids to bring back for a vase. What a pleasure to carry an armful of orchids! We returned to a delicious supper of vegetable soup and then rode up to the Motmot's nest. The clouds had closed in, however, and it was raining. The little birds were at the entrance to the nest, but no sign of the adults.*

That day was special, but judging by the log not so very different from the rest. Still, the week before had apparently been a rough one. I see a reference to "unpleasant" and to the "depressing efforts" to photograph the Cloud Swifts. That's handled in one of Jay's columns. (Very funny, Jay). Here's a list of what we photographed from blinds during the week of the log, usually with nest and young included: Rusty Sparrow, blue and white mockingbird, Brown-backed Solitaire, Southern House Wren, White napped Brush Finch, a flycatcher, Painted Redstart, Golden Browed Warbler, Rufous-capped Warbler, Wood- creeper, Blue-throated Motmot, Black Chachalaca, Black-headed Siskins, Slate-throated Redstart, Clay-colored Robin (which turned out to be an Orange-billed Nightingale-thrush, that according to the log "called like a Siamese cat and showed a pink-orange bill, gray breast, reddish back and something strangely colorful about the eye."), Yellow-faced Grassquit, and what may have been an Inca Dove. And those photographs were so beautiful they were like poems. Should I say here what happened to the collection? No, I won't quite yet.

We headed off for home the same way we arrived—in our homemade Volkswagen bus camper with bunks, stove and ice chest, and Harrington in his pup tent. While in Mexico we could just go anywhere. The people had such beautiful manners—thanking you for any little thing. Lovely people. If we asked to camp they always said yes and would visit with us far into the night and be back in the morning. I never felt in danger as long as we were in the country.

But Mexico City was another matter. We stopped there to shop and the city was full of thieves and the traffic—twelve lanes of traffic with the only rule being "if you could make it, you could make it." It was against the law to hit anybody—which led finally to my only bargain ever with God. "God, if you let us out of this place, I'll never come back." I never did.

And as a bonus, we had a pleasant experience next. Driving up the Pacific coast we came to this gorgeous deserted beach. We realized we were on someone's ranch and asked the first person we saw if we could stay. He said, "Oh, no." He said the owner would not want us camping on the beach. He would want us to come in and use the guest house.

So we did.

The owner owned 17 miles of beach. This was a tremendous cattle ranch. And the owner arrived the next day, the most aristocratic gentleman I'd ever met. He apologized that he could not be a better host but his wife was not there and the house servants had been given a holiday. We started this conversation in our pidgin Spanish until he suggested we switch to English. His English was perfect. He invited us to the roundup the following day.

The cowboys rounded up the cattle to milk them. They sat on little three legged milking stools that were made of silver. A paradise. Big foamy pitchers of milk for everyone to drink. And the cowboy's clothing had all this silver trim—buckles everywhere and ornately cut boots with silver spurs jangling. Then tens of thousands of parakeets began to settle in around the cattle. Flowers and bananas were growing everywhere and the sky was just dense with these yellow and purple and red parakeets collapsing in among the cattle.

On top of all that we were staying in a guest house with fresh towels and soap and plumbing and real beds to sleep in. A paradise.

Home at last. Jay had been planning that trip for years—studying the Mexican birds ahead of time—and now he had succeeded. We carried the slides to a Wilson Club meeting in Charleston. We showed them to a very enthusiastic audience and then went into the next room for a banquet. A couple from Florida approached us and offered to buy the slides. Jay said, "Oh, no. This project is something I planned for half of my life. I'm so proud of them, I couldn't possibly sell even one." When we came back from dinner every slide was gone. Every single one. All the originals. We had held back a few of the imperfect shots, but I suppose the heat in the attic has destroyed even those by now. Nothing was ever published. All those Mexican birds—those photographs were like poems they were so beautiful. It makes you wonder.

(Doe Hall, S.C. 2000)

JAY: Mexico 1961

Swifts

A Chimney Swift turned in flight 200 feet above our Greenville home, and mentally I noted April 2 as the first observation of this spring. With that peculiar wing beat resembling the stroke of oars, he went on his way and left me standing on the lawn—with my own thoughts soaring off in two directions. Looking ahead four months to August, Martha and I hoped to be in the jungles of Peru where the Swifts spent the winter. And if things went well, we'd be back in the South Carolina foothills before the swifts returned to Peru in October.

The second thought skipped back ten years to a limestone cliff in southern Mexico. A waterfall gushed out of a hole 100 feet up the wall. At some time in the dim past, the flow of water must have been greater, for the underground stream fell from a slot cut in the floor of a round tunnel above—a perfect keyhole in the rock.

What attracted me were Cloud Swifts zipping in and out of the hanging cave. They were twice as big as the Swifts at home and were flying straight back into the core of the mountain.

A series of cracks zigzagged toward the entrance. Over Martha's objections, I climbed the 100 feet up, and once in the slot from which the water poured, had little trouble working my way to the tunnel's mouth. Then going in, I walked in the dim light 500 feet upstream and reached a circular chamber where another waterfall entered high on the right.

Swifts were clinging to the walls of this subterranean room. Here was a chance to photograph a bird usually seen high overhead. I went out to the cliff, descended, and picking up what was necessary, returned. Or tried to. The equipment was so heavy I kept peeling off the mountainside. I repacked, assigning some of the load to Martha. She decided she would as soon climb with me as stay below and watch me fall. Struggling every inch, we labored together. We felt for toe and handholds, decided we couldn't cross a particular gap and then decided that we had to—until finally we gained the safety of the tunnel's shoulder.

Martha sat down on the shelf. Not noticing how ancient currents had cut beautiful wave patterns into the surface, she began to cry. After some time, she was finally able to speak. She told me that here she would die for there was no way she could ever get back down.

"Go ahead and photograph the swifts—you might as well," she said. "Then come back and tell me goodbye."

Once more in the dark chamber, I discovered that mist from the waterfall soaked my equipment and short-circuited my lights. A wire broke in the cord that connected lights to camera. Efforts to take pictures were frustrated at every turn. Still, it was quite a sight—the black and white birds coming and going in an underground environment that exceeded the powers of imagination. By the time I returned Martha had collected herself. We lowered the camera pack with a coil of clothesline I happened to have along and, without a slip, picked our way to the rocks below.

But going to the Tetons a few years later, we discovered that no sensible mountain climber would have attempted such a climb without all sorts of safety aids and that our 100 foot cliff would rank at the top in degrees of difficulty. So, Martha, I promise you, if we get to the Amazon this summer you won't have to climb any cliffs or penetrate any underground streams. Some rapids and maybe a whirlpool or two, but only if taking good pictures makes it absolutely necessary.

(Greenville, S.C. 1970)

Martha: When the time came to go to Peru, Jay went alone. This was the spring of 1971. He decided the trip would be just too much for me—and it was almost too much for him. When he got into the Amazon basin the intestinal microbes caught up with him and the going got very rough.

JAY: Peru, 1971

Mother and child

Four years old, or maybe five, she stood her ground as I, camera in hand, climbed toward the ridge. She had responsibilities. A baby was strapped to her back and she kept her eyes on a band of rooting pigs, as well. She was a child of the Altiplano tribe where the closest a little girl comes to playing is to wash clothes in a cold stream, dig potatoes or take charge of mother's baby. And I, climbing in the thin air of that 14,000 foot altitude and burdened with equipment, was a heavily breathing, strangely dressed aberration at least twice as big as any man in her village. The four-year-old became a child after all. She retreated a few steps and set up a plaintive wail.

If anything distresses me it is to make a little girl cry. I edged over the ridge and came into view of the adults harvesting potatoes. In bright but dusty costumes, they chopped the ground with hand hoes and sorted out what they uncovered. But two apart were preparing lunch—heaping potatoes onto heated stones.

The crop they were gathering was not some horticultural invention brought in by a foreign expert, but one of their many contributions to the world's agriculture. And who could say? Perhaps the first potato was brought under cultivation in this very field, a little terraced acreage which seemed to hang in that sky of deep blue—where luminous clouds were expanding. One abruptly blotted out the sun.

The Indians stopped work and gathered for lunch in the lee of adjacent boulders. Hard, rattley pellets of snow began to fall. They pulled blankets close about their shoulders.

The coca leaf of the Inca's is said to ease wary muscles and ward off the cold. One of the men took the dried green leaves from a bag and gave each (including the children) a handful. They chewed until their mouths ran with green saliva and their smiles widened.

Then the potatoes were divided, and I, too, was offered my share. But sad to say, I had to decline for the local strain of intestinal flora has not been domesticated, at least by me.

The pigs moved in—apparently liking cooked potatoes better than raw. The big sow squealed when her nose touched a hot rock.

The mother untied the baby from her little girl's back, settled carefully against a boulder, and began to nurse. Bright tiny fragments of snow rolled over her straight black hair, to melt on the exposed breast and the face of the hungry infant.

(Huancoyo, Peru 1971)

Music

My driver and I had come as high as the road would take us. A tier of dark mountains shaded by a bank of gray clouds rimmed the horizon. And then we realized that above the gray clouds, were not white clouds, but mountains higher still— jagged, distant, and even colder.

Where we stood the wind blew cold. Potato fields and flocks of sheep had been left behind several layers below. Nothing grew in this frigid zone of the Altiplano but puna, the grass pasturage of the alpaca herds, and patches of snuggled-together cactus as white and wooly as polar bears. So we were surprised to hear through the thin air the toot- toot-toot and hurump-rump-rump of a small brass band. Following the music down the road for about a mile, we found its source.

To escape the wind, the three Quechua musicians were settled in a sheltering hole, one perhaps dug by lama herdsman a 1000 years ago—and only their heads and the polished bells of their instruments showed above ground level. Now, politely pretending that we had not intruded, they continued to work on a particularly difficult passage, playing over and over the same sequence of notes.

Finally, came a pause, and my driver Anticona greeted them. Soon we were all engaged in a lively conversation, for the isolation of the plateau encouraged this. Then the discussion ended and they offered to play a song. The tune was not familiar. The trumpet kept coming in on each phrase a half-beat before the base instruments and lingering a sliding half-beat longer. The music was happy and complicated and like the musicians who played it, young.

They stopped. We thanked them profusely and they thanked us for happening along to serve as audience. But they didn't need us. Not really. As we drove away, they played on—like birds making music for themselves and for the sky.

We traveled miles before we came to other people. A shepherd stood in the puna teaching his young son to use a sling—the type David used to slay Goliath.

(Huancoyo, Peru 1971)

The Universe

A philosopher friend told me of a sage who urged his pupils to truly understand a tiny part of something and then they would understand it all. My friend bravely expanded this statement to include the entire universe, but I'd be content if my fiddler crab observations simply suggested some broader insight into their salt marsh home.

As soon as Martha and I got our possessions stored under a low country roof (they looked as woe-be-gone as a hermit crab evicted from his shell), I went out to the fiddler colony.

Like African antelope in miniature they grazed on the flats recently abandoned by the ebbing tide. As for grazing—with their tiny claws they shoveled sand into one side to their mouths, skimmed off algae growing on the grains, and spit cleansed particles out of the other. The algae had been nourished by decaying marsh grass, now each fiddler in turn can nourish the fish, birds and mammals that waited toward the top of the energy pyramid. A smaller group hung behind on a low mound pocked with mud-marqueed burrow entrances. At each doorway a mature male waved his big claw vigorously. When another male ventured too close, the two locked claws in a push and shove battle (again, not unlike the antelope). A female wandered over the crest, and immediately the males shifted attention from combat to courtship. They tip-toed and fiddled desperately. But fiddlers, like insects, have compound eyes, excellent for perception of depth and movement, poor for seeing detail.

The female they lavished this attention on had already mated, and now waddled heavy with well developed eggs. Probably, she was even then on her way to the retreating water to dampen the 10 to 30 thousand potential offspring tucked under her belly in a spongy, mahogany-red mass.

The fiddling fiddlers may have been disappointed in her lack of response, but I was pleased to see her. Breeding season ends early in September, and I had wondered if I'd find a gravid female to photograph and study at this late date.

Obviously, fiddlers lead complicated lives. And even more complicated are the workings of their marvelously productive salt marsh home—of which the entire mysterious universe is in part composed.

(Greenville, S.C. 1972)

Fiddlers

Rising from the bed of the stream, a concealed blue crab ambushed the adventuring male fiddler. Perhaps the victim was the same hapless soul I studied a few days earlier. Considering the size of the colony, what were the odds—a thousand to one?

An adult male worked diligently to dig out the burrow a tide had collapsed. He came out regularly with a load, a neat ball of sand. Judging by the pile that accumulated at his door, he was making real progress.

But his was the misfortune to be neighbor to an adolescent male, one just beginning his fiddling career. The youngster thought it great sport to fiddle his larger claw back and forth before his better—who deigned not to notice. Still, every time the working male backed into his hole for another load, the young scamp, took this as retreat, and dashed up madly waving his red-jointed appendage. Then, swaggering in his success, he waited to deliver a new flurry of fiddler nose-thumbing the moment the older male re-emerged.

Finally, the adult lost patience. With one sweep of his massive claw he sent the youngster tumbling. He did not bother to follow up his advantage; that should be lesson enough. He crawled back for more sand.

But Red-claw was not the least chastised. He returned and pushed half of the hard-dug sand down the hole. When nothing happened, he boldly pushed the rest in. Then he dug some new sand and added that to the top. I thought the burrow was blocked, but soon the adult pushed out, plowing loose sand in front and pulling a freshly dug ball behind. He paused and faced his young neighbor. Neither moved. Perhaps they communicated. Hostilities were about to end. For now.

At this point I called to Martha to bring her red fingernail polish so I might mark their claws for future observation—I would trace the progress of this feud. That didn't work. Within an hour the polish had rubbed off on the abrasive sand. Experiment ended.

But not the broader observation of fiddler life. That male taken by the blue-crab probably wasn't the same I'd watched fencing with his young rival, but no doubt, on better days the mealtime victim had experienced much the same. And now his end had come—in part. The food he had consumed and made into his body had moved up to another level—and not all of it in the stomach of the ravenous crab. As that crab had done his work, a dozen tiny fish had darted eagerly around. The crab's claws were occupied. The fish snatched up scraps of fiddler that drifted away in the lazy current.

(Doe Hall, S.C. 1971)

The Big Bang

Gazing into such a sky one has the feeling he can see forever but according to current scientific thinking, probably the limits of the universe cannot exceed 18 billion light years away. With my middle-aged, albeit far-sighted, eyes I can see only a fraction that far.

Perhaps, without knowing it, I glimpsed one of the galaxies that has stirred the astronomic fraternity to fierce debate. A few of these learned men and women have retreated from the conventional position that 18 billion years ago the universe began with a "big bang" of an infinitely compressed black body that has been expanding ever since.

The rebel scientists reject the notion that the background radiation spreading evenly throughout space originated from the ancestral black body.

They claim they have evidence that some galaxies may be moving at speeds greater than the speed of light, contradicting Einstein's relativity, and some galaxies that establishment scientists say are far separated and sailing toward the outer bounds at different speeds, actually are close together, connected by luminous jets of gas.

The mavericks think this means that a new physics may be aborning, opening windows on worlds and systems yet undreamed of. They wonder if relativity will prove only a crude approximation of cosmological affairs, if matter, instead of originating with a single big bang deep in the astronomical past, may even now be created and consumed in many cells of the honeycomb of existence. Shocking ideas!

Just to stand on the edge of the marsh looking at the bright pinpoints in the midnight sky makes my head spin. I hope scientists will get together soon and explain to me what's going on out there.

(Doe Hall, S.C. 1972)

SMALL LOVE

I took our love and measured it and found
That though it fails to circle the whole Earth
We are encompassed, and together bound.
We would feel lost in love of greater girth
Our love does not flash boldly as a star
Exposed to all the watchers of the night.
The glow we share may not be seen afar,
But for the two of us its shine is bright.

I have heard lovers cry, "Infinity
Does not define the boundaries of our love."
Poor souls. I offer them my sympathy.
The love I know is finite as a glove.
Our small warm love is much too dear to waste
Diffused and chilled through all of outer space.

From: A confidence on Parting

MARTHA: A New House, 1973

We were moving away from Greenville. Jay was driving a U-Haul van and I was driving the Volkswagen. And it began to rain—sheets of rain that the little windshield wipers just slapped at. I was crying, as well. I couldn't see a thing. I was leaving behind so many good friends, I just wept and wept. Finally, I had to make a bargain with God. My second bargain since I had made a similar one down in Mexico City. I told God he must either make the rain stop or make me stop crying because I couldn't continue to look through both tears and raindrops. So God made the rain stop. I guess that was easier.

This was 1973 and we had decided to move back to the coast, back to the McClellanville area where we'd been born and raised. Jay was doing well with the filmstrips and we felt we could live pretty much where we wanted. I asked Daddy for a piece of his family's property at Doe Hall. This was part of an old plantation, several hundred acres on the Intracoastal Waterway—mostly pine and hardwood forest but with some fields and across the front was a tremendous duck pond. The pond was salt marsh and beyond that was broad Bull's Bay which bordered the ocean. I asked Daddy and he said, sure. He'd give us five acres. He said just walk over the land and pick a spot.

Along the pond edge it was pretty thick. I remember Jay climbing a tree and selecting our site with that view in mind. Later he said we picked it because a swallowtail kite was gliding around. That's possible. We once bought a piece of mountain property because an orchid was growing on it—growing in a spring—and it came with an abandoned swimming pool filled with humus and other mountain plants.

Eventually we sold that parcel to a nature conservancy group.

But for Doe Hall and the dream house: I had an architect friend, Bobby Foster, that I'd gone to school with and we asked him to help. He and Jay sat down on the living room sofa and designed a house that just gave Daddy a fit. This was a fairly modern post and beam house. A tremendous triangular shaped brick chimney went soaring up in the middle of a 40-foot wide hexagonal room and off that was a bedroom and bath for us and at the other end a guest room and bath contained in a smaller hexagonal. And a deck went practically all the way round the house and at one point even through the house.

Well, Daddy had expected an antebellum columned plantation house. But Jay and I wanted what our architect Bobby had drawn. Which in the end didn't matter because we decided we didn't really have the money for such a house. By which time daddy had decided he really liked our plan and offered to give us the foundation—45 pilings 25 feet long and driven into the ground—driving piling was what his and my brother Horry's company often did. So we started and Daddy would climb up there 12 feet in the air and wander around where the flooring was now framed up. He had glaucoma and could hardly see. We made him stop so he sent his old crony Buck Marlowe to supervise and after a couple of weeks Jay convinced them both that he was up to the job.

We had hired Junior Simmons, a local carpenter. Junior was black and totally self taught. He told Jay once that he'd been rolling a wheelbarrow on a job back in the late 40's and kept watching the carpenters out of the corner of his eye. Then he just went out and bought a hammer, saws, and framing square. He had his two nephews for helpers. I'm not sure they had ever built a full-sized house before. But he said he could do it and he could. He had an incredible work ethic—hardly ever took a break. Jay just sat there in the middle of the platform and interpreted the plan which was actually no more than elevations and a floor plan. This great spider web of beams 19 feet up in the air and going every which way was something Junior just had to figure out. And he didn't ask Jay for help very often—except I do remember at the end when they got to a circular wooden stairway. Junior asked for help then because Jay wanted everything hanging in space with these curious cutouts in the rail. They laughed over that.

Building the house took a full year. They had a good time, Jay and Junior. And the resulting house had the best vibes. It was like a great, multi-layered homemade cake, one that's not quite perfect but a happy cake—a comfortable made-from-scratch cake—a delicious house. Cypress paneling on the inside and outside. Oak floors and lots of tile and marble. Jay insisted on a Japanese soaking tub made out of green marble that, like everywhere else in the house, would have a view of the pond and salt marsh. The tub fixture, the water spigot, was almost as expensive as the tub so my brother Sonny donated a big conch shell. I was walking behind the plumber. He didn't know it and kept muttering "Goddamn conch shell."

Now there was a downside. Jay, Bobby, Daddy, Junior—everybody seemed to have input on that house but me. From the beginning Jay had insisted that only one person could build a house and that we'd never get it done unless we did it his way. Still, I made suggestions. We liked to swim in the salt water creek next to the pond so I asked for a shower under the house. Jay said the pipes would freeze. I asked for a garbage disposal. Jay agreed and then said it would mess up the septic tank and took it out. Finally, I just had to say, you build it and I'll look when you're finished.

And as wonderful and livable as that house was on one level, on another it was impossible. The insulation was only Styrofoam two inches thick and with those high ceilings the house was completely unheatable and uncoolable. And the plumbing was always freezing and never worked even before it froze. Then after we went back in the Park Service, we rented the house out. Puppies chewed the doors, wasp nests everywhere, woodpeckers pecking, and always the plumbing freezing again and again.

But such a view. The house had been designed around that view of the pond and the marsh. You were 12 feet up in the air and from every room and from the deck you could look out on this 20-acre ever-changing pond and beyond that the incredible expanse of marsh and sky. And ocean. On rough days you could see the surf breaking across the front of the bay. And right up beside the house Daddy dug a little canal that we really didn't want. We preferred things to be natural, but he dug it and then had his buddy Buck Marlowe wade out and plant water lilies while he stood on the bank and shouted directions. Both men were deaf. White water lilies everywhere.

In September of 1989 we lost that house. The way we found out the house was gone was that after Hurricane Hugo I reached my sister Emily on the telephone. She and Oran had found refuge in Columbia. Sonny and Hazel had built a house on five acres next to ours and they had stayed there during the storm. Emily didn't mention them and when I did, she said she was hoping I wouldn't ask. She'd heard nothing. We knew from the national television bulletins how bad the storm had been—winds up to 150 miles an hour and an 18 foot storm surge. We both thought Sonny and Hazel must be dead. Then I managed to get the Frampton's in Mt. Pleasant on the phone. They were my nephew Michael's in-laws. And just as they answered Sonny and Hazel walked through their door—looking like drowned rats.

When Sonny realized that their house might not survive, they had taken the two dogs and driven out to the elementary school on the highway. They had a thermos of coffee and the clothes on their backs. They parked there. Sonny counted 70 tornadoes and even on that rise a mile from the coast the water covered their truck tires. They slept a few hours and at dawn walked back to the house sites. Their house was gone. Our house was gone. The house that Oran had just built for Emily and himself was gone.

With that kind of loss comes an incredible sense of disorientation. Years later, Jay would say "That went in the hurricane"—even if the missing object hadn't. Sonny and Hazel found most of their silverware and cut glass pitcher and glasses that had come from Mama. A young family, the Sisson's, was renting from us and they picked up some of our treasures in the woods. Jay had carried his Audubon prints and William Zimmerman paintings with us out West. And I'd carried my silver and Mama's tea service. We had carried most of the slides. The Sisson's found my wedding crystal still packed in a box and wrapped in tissue—sitting in the mud. Mama's old secretary was gone. Our nine-foot banquet table was gone. Myra Davis had given me a beautiful chest of drawers and two wing chairs. The chest was found with the veneer completely curled up. The chairs were gone. But the two sofas were sitting off in the woods like it was a sylvan parlor—but both beyond repair. Everything in this present house is second hand. My nephew James gave and lent us some pieces. We went to the thrift stores.

But Sonny and Hazel and Emily and Oran were alive. In the McClellanville shelter at the public high school hundreds of people had almost drowned but didn't. Sonny and Hazel built back. Em and Oran decided to stay in Mama and Daddy's house in the village. And Jay and I built this much smaller and more practical house on some of the first house's pilings. We had to go another four feet in the air, so the view is the same or better and my entire electric bill for last month was $28.00. Jay and I were quite snug here and now I'm snug alone.

(Doe Hall, S.C. 2001)

Martha: That first year in the new house, 1973, Jay and I watched this odd weather front moving across the bay towards us in our brand new house. He said, "That's snow, Mart." It was. A freak storm that left us with eight inches on the ground—our "house warming."

JAY: Snow

Like many pioneers of old, Evening Grosbeaks thrive in new territory, for they, too, know how to exploit an unused but common habitat. Indeed, ground modified by man figures in the success of most of our bird immigrants—House Sparrows, House Finches, Starlings and Cattle Egrets to name the most obvious.

During the Great Southern Blizzard last weekend, Evening Grosbeaks, showed how thoroughly they have learned the uses of man. Saturday morning, as on signal, these recent immigrants from the Northwest deserted wild ice-covered fruit and mast-bearing trees and swooped out of the woods. In short order they had checked out the houses, rejected those that had no feeding stations and settled in mass on those that did.

By now every Grosbeak knows that many people feed birds so a house may be a landmark against starvation, and in the grosbeak's year, winter is that time of testing. A few sunflower seeds can make all the difference, and not just to the Evening Grosbeaks. Few species are so solitary they do not investigate a flock of birds suddenly busy in one spot. They arrived at our feeders flashing white, yellow and black feather signals across the icy landscape, and within minutes the cowbirds had arrived, as well. Then Redwings, Grackles and Blue Jays. They poured in—Starlings, Towhees, Juncos, Fox Sparrows and Fish Crows.

Even birds that never eat seed came to investigate. Robins prodding ground unfrozen near our flowing-well were joined by Snipe and then a Glossy Ibis was pushing his curved beak into that patch of soft earth.

But for Martha and me the most curious and handsome sighting was a single Common Egret. With white plumes as delicate as snowflakes, he parachuted softly down to a snowdrift. He strode elegantly to the suet and with his rapier beak, broke off a piece. He started to swallow, but changed his mind—for the suet must not have seemed as slippery as a fish. He took his prize to a snow pool, dipped it in the icy water several times and with a gulp and shudder, the properly prepared suet began like a bobbing Adam's apple on the journey down his long neck.

(Doe Hall, S.C. 1973)

MARTHA: Harrington and Miss Mary's Illness, 1974-1982

As I mentioned, Mama grew up in Grahamville which is down close to the border at Savannah. She was the oldest of nine children and was teaching school for $35 a month. She paid $10 a month for a horse and buggy, $10 a month for room and board and sent $10 home to her mother, and kept the rest for extravagances. She had taught in several small towns and when she finally got up to McClellanville, Daddy fell in love with her at once. Of course, the local girls were outraged.

But Daddy proposed to this Mary Horry from Grahamville. She declined. Again and again, he asked. Finally, she agreed to marry him if he would (1) become an Episcopalian (2) give her a diamond ring, and (3) finish the house he had started out at the Bellefield farm. Well, he'd already spent the diamond ring money on a Model T. Ford and the house wasn't finished so they had to spend the first few months living with his parents. But he did become an Episcopalian. He'd go. He'd hum the first hymn and then nod off for the rest of the service—which was standard for most of the men—maybe even above average.

That little cabin he built was rolled the four miles into McClellanville and is the basis for the house that my sister Emily and her husband Oran live in today. The farming at Bellefield had failed so he went into the turpentine business and then got cypress piling out of the Santee River swamps and ended up joining his father in a new construction business. The foundation of the old Cooper River Bridge rests on Daddy's cypress pilings. When I'd drive him over it to see the doctor, he'd tease me about those "little saplings"—especially if the traffic stalled with us at the top.

Mother married him and they lived in McClellanville and were happy. But when Jay and I returned in 1973 and I got on the Episcopal altar guild, I asked her a question about the duties. She answered, "You'll have to ask Mrs. Lucas. I'm a newcomer here." She wasn't joking. She and Daddy had been married over fifty years when she told me that. Another time we were having Christmas dinner. Daddy was in his bed dying, so the whole family fit in that little bedroom and sang the Doxology before going into dinner. "Praise God from whom all blessings flow." This was sung by a family of 30 around the bed. Then we all went in to Christmas dinner. Someone leaned over to Mother and said something like, "What a wonderful Christmas." She replied, "And not one of my family is with us." Of course, we were all her family—all thirty—children and grandchildren and great grandchildren. But what she meant was none of her own brothers and sisters was there.

When Daddy could still get around, he and I kept a three-acre garden. Each year Mama and I would put up what we'd grown—can or freeze it. We did this on our deck. I'd serve Daddy a little bourbon and branch and then lunch. When Emily moved back, she wasn't enthusiastic about any of this. One morning we canned all the snap beans and canned all the tomatoes and froze the butter beans. Everything was done—it seemed. Daddy leaned back in his chair, took a sip of his drink, and announced, "There's nothing left to put up except the pears." Emily, who never ever takes the Lord's name in vain, said, "Pears! I'm not putting up one goddamn pear!" The next week we were putting up pears. She couldn't stay away. She would have missed the fun of snapping beans with Mama and hearing Daddy talk. And the next spring she was anxious to plant—confessing to me that those put up vegetables were the best she'd ever tasted.

I grew up with a great sense of family—that the family comes first. Once Em and I had come back and as long as Mother and Daddy lived we would all get together for Sunday dinner. My brother-in-law and my sisters-in-law were very much a part of Mama and Daddy's family. And today we are bound by this family loyalty. It gives us all strength. We're all there for each other

When Daddy was sick the last time, he came home from the hospital and said to Emily and me, he said, "I don't want to go back there. Will you two please let me die in this same bed I was born in?" That was the big four poster that had come out of the famous Edmundson-Alston house in Charleston.

We said we would if the doctors agreed. The doctors said yes. They said he's ready to go. They taught Emily and me how to give morphine shots. When Daddy died Mama was sitting beside him in her wheel chair and Em and I were on either side of him each holding a hand. We told him we loved him. He stopped breathing. He was quiet. Mama said, "Will you let me go like that?"

I looked after the two of them for ten years. At first with just the housekeeper, Louetta Brown, then with Emily when she and Oran returned from Charlotte. We had a little hospital. Daddy died. Mama could still get up and walk to the living room. A week before she died Em and I took her to the beauty parlor. She loved a day in the beauty shop. Then I went in with breakfast and she shook her head and wouldn't open her mouth. She wouldn't talk. She didn't eat or talk for a week. She just looked at us. We had called the doctors and they said she was telling us to let her go—to let her die. We would swab her lips. She didn't say another word. The last words she'd said—on that morning she had stopped talking—one word, really—was "handsome." I went into her room, opened the window and put feed on the bird feeder just outside. A blue jay came. Mama turned to me and said, "Handsome." She never said another word. When she died Em and I were there and our younger brother Horry. But Sonny just couldn't bear losing her. He came just after she was gone.

Those years together of nursing Mama and Daddy enhanced the bond of love between Em and me. We are extremely close. She's an angel and I thank God every day for her.

I've been thinking again about the trip to Oregon and Mama riding with me down that slippery mountain road with Jay out in the snow pushing to keep the car from plunging over the side. And Mama said, "Where is the snake?" She wept because I had left my little Pacific boa behind.

Long years after that, Jay had ordered some snakes and I had to go out to the Greenville Airport. This meant driving from Blowing Rock, North Carolina. The snakes were coming in from Florida. When I got to the airport the man said, "Go out there and get them because I don't think I can get anybody to bring them to you." We went back into this big hanger warehouse and he pointed into the corner. The box (without lid) was marked "Dangerous Reptiles—Handle with Care." The snakes were in the box tied up in croaker sacks. A Cottonmouth and Canebrake rattler and several others Jay wanted to photograph. I carried them back to the Blue Ridge Parkway. We had a tiny trailer that Mama was staying in. Harrington was sleeping outside in his hammock and Jay and I had pitched a little tent. One night it started to rain. I heard Mama whisper, "Jay...Jay...Jay." She was calling from the door of the trailer. He answered, "Yes, mother-in-law." She said, "It's raining." He said, "Yes, I hear it." She said, "How about the snakes? Are they going to be all right out there in that croaker sack?" He said, "Yes, mother-in-law. They're cold-blooded animals and the rain suits them fine." She said, "Oh, all right."

That was the relationship they had. One of pure love. Which I suppose is why Em and I could take up with the two motherless boys we married in the first place. Mama took them in too and they both loved her so.

(Doe Hall, S.C. 2000)

JAY: The End of Winter

A Cardinal

This morning, Spring was announced by the song of a Cardinal. Not by the arrival of a Robin.

Robins live in the Carolina Foothills all year long, and with flocks moving in from the north each fall, Robins are more common in winter than any other season. True, they're not conspicuous for most wander in flocks over plowed fields and pasture. They move from holly to ligustrum, from golf course to interstate median. Occasionally one does walk across a lawn—where he is noticed and reported as the first Robin of Spring—though it might still be December. Ecologists say that spring is actually two seasons. (A famous ecologist once defined ecology as the incomprehensible taught by the incompetent. Recruited now into the vocabulary of politics, that definition of the word takes on new strength.) Early spring differs from late spring as much as summer differs from fall, or fall from winter.

Certainly by mid-February many life processes, suspended since October, begin to stir again. Peach orchards blush deeper with swelling buds than they will when pink blossoms unfold. On south slopes where bare trees allow the sun to stream in, porcelain-blue hepatica flowers appear. In forest pools amphibian eggs are found in clusters—like crystalline grapes, one black seed in the center of each.

Dead leaves pulled aside reveal new poison ivy shoots, vigorous and seeped with ivy oil—more potent than in summer. The proof: blisters on my hands from that day we looked at Golden Mouse nests.

Yes, days are still shorter than nights, but the sun rises earlier and lingers til after six.

Yes, when Late Spring brings breaks in the ice and a flood of green strewn with wild flowers sweeps across the Foothills, that is spectacular. But early spring has one great advantage. It comes first—announced by the Cardinal's song.

Valentines Day and the male Cardinals break the winter silence with their musically simple but firmly stated song. With a hundred notes and as many cadences, an April Mockingbird paints a detailed picture in sound. The February Cardinal suggests more with a few mellow lines. Theirs is the tuning of the orchestra, the one scheduled in late spring to perform the daily choruses of dawn. To make up for the early spring silences of other birds, the female Cardinals sing, as well—but wait a few days til their mates have firmly established the season.

Of course, we who listen are subject to prejudice and preconception. We think the hen Cardinal's song less brilliant, more subdued. But at times she will sing in that elusive whisper, music that seems to come from far away. Listen. Introspective music, thought more than voice.

(Greenville, S.C. 1970)

MARTHA: In Later Years

After leaving Greenville, Jay and I did keep having adventures. But once down on the coast at Doe Hall, he started running the ferry to nearby Bull's Island and was pretty much tied down. He carried mostly birders and tourists and spent all day out on this long barrier island famous for birding. I was nursing Mama and Daddy. After seven years he gave up the tour boat—at which point his partner, who had never done anything, sued us and that case dragged on for years. Jay tried a bus tour. He would pick up tourists in Charleston and take them birding around here and bring them to our house for a glass of sherry and on to see the plantations and churches. People loved it, but still we couldn't manage the insurance, van payments and hours spent on the road. And so Jay went back to work with the Park Service—which is what he wanted to do anyway.

But I should back up. In the late 70's Jay had become involved in preserving a wilderness area inside the Francis Marion National Forest—this tremendous acreage that bordered us. The particular piece, called I'On Swamp, was about to be cut. Not a virgin forest, of course. Some of the swamp was a long abandoned inland rice field, now filled with grand trees—but all of it, a well-established and beautiful swamp and forest. A decade earlier, Jay had spotted and taken the last photograph of a Bachman's warbler. (Several recent books on vanishing species mention this proof but all leave out Jay's name.) That photo was taken not far from I'On Swamp, and in 1973 two of our friends had spotted the bird there—which was the last sighting in the United States. Since this was the last known habitat of this endangered species, Jay and his associates in the environmental organizations were able to stop the Forest Service from cutting and eventually to have I'On Swamp designated as a Wilderness Area. Which actually, turned out happily for the at-first-reluctant Forest Service. After Hurricane Hugo destroyed most of their old growth timber, the Francis Marion received a more tourist friendly, naturalist friendly director and I'On Swamp became their best advertised and most visited nature area.

Naturally, this pleased Jay, but he had another reward. Doing the historical research to support the environmentalists' claims, he began to read about the antebellum Lutheran minister John Bachman. Audubon had first spotted the new bird in a tupelo tree south of Charleston and named it in Bachman's honor, for when Audubon arrived in Charleston in search of birds to paint, Bachman befriended him. Both were avid naturalists and would go on to collaborate on several projects—including the marriage of Audubon's two sons to Bachman's two daughters.

Though much had been written about Audubon, little mention was made of this friendship, and Jay began a book *Had I the Wings* which was eventually published by the University of Georgia. Though Audubon and Bachman were very close friends and accomplished many things, Bachman was dismayed, especially towards the end of their lives, by Audubon's lack of discipline.

Jay spent years researching their friendship and discovered all sorts of involvements. Bachman's sister-in- law painted backgrounds for Audubon and both men were in love with her. Both of Bachman's daughters died after they married Audubon's sons. Such painful tragedy and such romance. That book is still in print. Jay identified with Bachman I think that's safe to say.

(Doe Hall, S.C. 2001)

JAY

From: Had I the Wings

Birds invaded Bachman's study. He had wondered if bobwhites could be bred in captivity, which aviculturists before him had tried and failed. Hatched by a bantam hen, several of his bobwhites became so tame they trailed the pastor about the garden and followed him into the study. When Bachman settled at his desk to write, as he did almost every day from four to eight in the morning, the most confiding of the quails settled beside him and nibbled his fingers. If he laid his pen on his desk to free his hand to rub his eyes, this bird would pick it up and scamper out of the door with it.

Originally housed in the aviary, a brown thrasher, which Audubon called a "Ferruginous Mocking-bird," was given the freedom of the garden. It learned to watch for Bachman to come outdoors with a spade in his hand. While Bachman dug, the thrasher lurked at his heels to snap up tidbits from the freshly-turned turf. It became so companionable it slept in the study perched on the back of Bachman's chair, the one with the wide arms that doubled as his writing table. When the study door was left ajar one evening, the vigilant Bachman cat slipped in and ate the thrasher.

A pair of pileated woodpeckers had better luck. Bachman kept them in his study from the summer of their capture as nestlings into the unusually cold winter that followed. Their home was a cage made of live oak as strong as iron. But the woodpeckers incessantly tested the bars, and one frigid dawn, the hour when Bachman habitually came to his desk to study and write undisturbed by his numerous household, he opened the door and a woodpecker flew from a shattered bookshelf and shot to freedom. The woodpecker left behind went on "hammering away" at Bachman's library as though the owner was not present. Bachman released it, too. Its wide wings cupped the cold air as it bounded to a garden tree where its cell mate waited. As though savoring their freedom, the pair hitched in step around the trunk, and as upon a secret signal took off and vanished into a landscape of smoking chimneys and walled gardens, pale under a rare Charleston dusting of snow.

(Had I the Wings, Univ. of Ga Press, 1995)

MARTHA: Back in the Park Service

After Daddy died, Jay started back in the Park Service on a part time basis up in Virginia at Otter Creek—and met an old time honey gatherer and his wife who still come to visit me. During this time Emily looked after Mama, and I would return to the coast and fill in some—give her a break. Then after Mama died, Jay and I spent three years at the Carl Sandburg Home Park in Flat Rock, North Carolina. Jay was the naturalist there.

In a way we were already connected to Flat Rock for this was the mountain resort where many low country planters had built their antebellum summer cottages—which were often mansions. Some of these had been from the McClellanville area, but my main connection was through Charleston. I sat in the Lowndes pew because I was kin to them. We were living already on Lowndes Lane and I became a bit like a daughter to the elderly Elizabeth Lowndes. I took her to church every Sunday and gave the bedridden Mr. I'On Lowndes his morphine shot—for I'd had plenty of practice with Daddy.

Anyway, Flat Rock was this very old fashioned aristocratic summer resort with solid white Victorian houses tucked away in mountainous laurel thick corners and between them tennis courts, golf courses, lakes, the slightly Gothic St. John's in the Wilderness Church—and thousands and thousands of perfect mountain acres to hike—and the Carl Sandburg Home National Historic Site—the house and farm that the Sandburg family had fairly recently donated to the country.

Jay was such a fan of Sandburg's this job was heaven sent for him. When Jay would recite the Chicago poem "City of Big Shoulders" for an audience up there, the Carl Sandburg people just wept. Jay could read Carl Sandburg's poetry better than Carl Sandburg, but maybe I am a bit prejudiced on that subject. Not long before the poet died, Jay had dinner with him—a thermos of goat's milk and honey for the poet, meatballs for Jay.

We were both friends with Sandburg's daughter Margaret who was a birdwatcher. And I knew Mrs. Sandburg who still kept goats and was delightful. The house was open to tours and was filled with the most charming furniture, all of it Sears Roebuck style which, since she was very down to earth, is exactly where it came from. Still, the Flat Rock establishment did feel Mrs. Sandburg should have redecorated before turning it over to the Park Service—which made no sense at all.

Only a few of the "nice" families had befriended the Sandburg's. The Lowndes had. But most people considered them to be sort of "peasants." And they were in a way. They kept goats. But then Sandburg's wife's brother was the photographer Edward Steichen and the house was filled with his photographs.

Sandburg would go up to the church's graveyard to write. He would sit on the graves and people didn't care for that—especially him sitting close to Colonel Rutledge's grave. Not on it, just close. Maybe because the poet had written the three-volume biography of Abraham Lincoln (I believe the sale of that allowed him to buy the Flat Rock estate) and Rutledge, "the boy Colonel", had naturally been a Confederate. I should add that like Jay and me, Rutledge had originally spent his summers in tiny McClellanville, which is where the Colonel's son Archibald, South Carolina's poet laureate, had been born. Maybe the oblique association to our own poet was the problem. Jay enjoyed both men's work and had done the illustrations for one of Archibald Rutledge's book—but to get back to Flat Rock.

Besides the graveyard, the other place Sandburg had gone to compose was a couple of miles away, a beautiful rock that offered a view of the entire valley. In the fall, especially, we would go up there for picnics—the entire staff would eat supper, watch the sun set, and come home in the dark. Incredibly beautiful. You couldn't help but love the Flat Rock area. Jay and

I rented the nicest apartment from the rector of the Episcopal Church, which was the small but long established St. John's in the Wilderness. Walter Roberts, the priest, had been at that church for 43 years. A brilliant man and totally neurotic. And a fine Biblical scholar. He and Jay, Jay who was the unbeliever, had happy if lengthy discussions on the subject. We all got on fine together, and Walter became my good friend which since he was a widower made all the elderly unattached ladies very jealous, especially since on the very first Sunday, he announced that my great-great-great-something grandfather's name was inscribed on the church bell tower.

Soon after that I found myself serving as Walter's unofficial hostess. I bought the flowers for his house and the groceries, and since Jay worked Sundays, I ate Sunday dinner with Walter and his family, children and grandchildren who still lived close by. I loved that church.

In Greenville we'd ended up having a terrible time. Our Episcopal minister became involved with some very wealthy church-going members of the John Birch Society. Their politics entered more and more into the services, until one Sunday, Jay went down and took Harrington out of what was no more than a far right indoctrination for children. I finally walked out in the middle of a sermon. But Flat Rock was completely different.

At first I volunteered to visit the older ladies in the congregation. But all three of them soon died which, since I had just lost my own parents, was distressing. I switched to the convalescent closet which was actually a building filled with hospital equipment that we loaned out—most often to the mountain people. For years the church's Lady's Society had been collecting dues and as their was no purpose for the money they decided to serve the community with health care aids, wheel chairs, hospital beds, walkers and the like.

The poorer people in that community hadn't been doing much except making corn liquor so they had no social security to speak of. I kept those records and got to meet all those interesting mountain people and also to act as the rector's hostess with a grand budget to spend on flowers and food for dinner parties and receptions that both Jay and I attended. Though Jay was close by, I suppose Walter did like me more than he should have.

Those were three years when I felt happy and energetic and good. We were near our Greenville friends again and Walter would let them use his guest room. Of course, we made new friends both inside the Park Service and out. And of course, Jay kept photographing and he was immersed in the Audubon/Bachman book. We had a tiny table to eat on and most of the surface was covered with a computer. Jay would type on that and I never understood it at all. I just thought it was the strangest contraption and it had Jay's complete attention. I would say do you want to hike? No. I've got to work. Work on the computer. I'd go off with the other hikers and have lots of fun. Those were happy years.

And Jay did make a substantial contribution to Sandburg scholarship—sort of. This is an entry from a journal he was keeping at the time.

(Doe Hall, S.C. 1999)

JAY: Journal, Feb. 8, 1982

Flat Rock

About a week ago I answered the parking lot phone. A deep throaty female voice, the type I associate with Mrs. Shipero of Miami (what ever happened to the Shiperos?). The lady said she had two guests with her who wanted to tour the house. She was of the local group who bring guests to Carl Sandburg Home to entertain them and consequently have toured the house many times themselves. As we moved along she politely would let me finish a room and if I left a seam in my talk into which she could wedge a remark, she would say, "But aren't you going to tell us about so and so?" When at last we got to Sandburg's upstairs study, and I worked through and concluded with the flashback about Charlie Sandburg getting only one orange on a hard time Christmas, my assistant guide said, "But aren't you going to tell us about the stove?" I said "What about the stove?" She said, "Sandburg brought it from Michigan packed full of cigar butts, and they are still in there. I think that's fascinating!"

I hadn't heard that story, so later I asked my boss Warren Weber about the butts in the stove. "Oh," he said, "That was just a joke someone played." which made no sense to me at all. What was funny about it? The only sensible thing I could come up with was that during Sandburg's last full summer (1966) he had used the stove as a convenient disposal container. Then, that winter he was sick and a fire was never lit to burn this all up. But when I opened the door of the stove I saw a flaw in my theory. A great mass of CHEWED butts had been put in at one time, supported by a couple of sheets from a magazine. Not much could be seen under the magazine sheets. Some more butts, some scraps of paper. Thoroughly curious, I asked Jim Eldridge, our curator (wrote down my interest on a card and handed it to him) and he said we would investigate and see if my theory that there might be documents underneath that might date the butts and shed light on their origin. About 3:30 yesterday we got together. Jim brought along a pair of insanely small white gloves and told me they were for me. I thought this was Jim's joke—some small child had lost them and he was laughing about my big hands. We went on up, a couple of cardboard boxes to receive the refuse and Jim lifted out the first batch. Pretty soon it began to look as though indeed the stove had been filled at a single time. After the first solid mass of butts, we began to find one butt, or two, or three, wrapped in a piece of newspaper or magazine. Some of the papers had dates—1864, as I remember was the most recent. The butts had been wet when wrapped, the papers were stained, no sign of ash. We began to find fewer butts and more papers. Quite a few empty envelopes—some with the return addresses of famous people. Johnathan Daniels, Andre Kartalanis. We found some sheets that had been torn up, the bits of handwriting obviously that of Sandburg. It was almost time to close up the house when Jim pulled out some pages folded to fit an envelope, and right next to them an envelope from someone in New York. They were all pressed flat, unrumpled, as though they had been squeezed into a crowded file. The sheets were each carbons of scatological verse. The poems were literate and dealt with religion, society and sex—with an almost school boyish zeal for profanity.

(Flat Rock, N.C. 1982)

MARTHA: On Sandburg's Poems: I'm not sure what they decided. Possibly those poems had been sent to Sandburg by an admiring imitator, but more likely they'd been written by the poet himself. Anyway, they were sent on to the Sandburg archives, and I don't think those never-before seen or heard-of verses have still been seen or heard by anybody but Jay and a few other park officials.

MARTHA: Badlands National Park

Wall's Drugstore is the largest drugstore in the world. In the early 1900's a young pharmacist opened a drug store in Wall, South Dakota—which was almost in the middle of nowhere. The second summer there, his wife suggested they put a sign out on the highway that said "Free Ice Water." They did and thereby a fortune was made. The drugstore ended up being a block long—maybe two blocks—and inside you find not just drugs but everything—in the world. They have an art gallery exhibiting excellent Western paintings. There's a chapel for getting married in, stuffed buffaloes, a mechanical chicken who lays eggs. She cackles with each egg and a mechanical band plays. One of Jay's interns told us he was getting on a bus in London and saw a sign saying how many miles it was to Wall's Drugstore.

But Jay and I were only 30 miles from Wall's. Jay went out to Badlands as Assistant Chief Naturalist and for the last three years was Chief Naturalist. He worked five days a week and for the other two we stayed in the park and photographed—except when we drove in to Wall's Drugstore and had a big breakfast or an even bigger lunch. We carried Ev and Tunks with us one day and Ted, the owner, stopped by for introductions. "Our aunt and uncle, Ev and Tunks." We were having our buffalo burgers and he stayed and chatted. And when we were done here came the chocolate nut sundaes with his compliments. He and his wife were good, good friends. Both have died now and their son runs "The Largest Drugstore in the World."

Badlands National Park was incredible. Really, an under appreciated park—something to do with being called "bad lands." We had a rainy season, but for the remainder the land was dry and cracked. Yet when the desert does bloom it's spectacular. Buffalo, mule deer, all sorts of animals. The South Carolina naturalist Rudy Mankee came out and made a television program there. And the fossils were everywhere. The superintendent's wife was a dear friend and she'd gone back to school just to learn the fossils. When Jay died she flew me out to Zion where they were stationed.

Once she and I found a large turtle that seemed to be stepping out of the rock. Millions of years old but stepping out. We showed it only to our husbands and made them swear never to tell. There were plenty enough fossils to show the visitors and thieves would have chiseled out that turtle. Jay's main job was to teach the interns. Occasionally, he might do an evening talk and slide show for someone who was off. But that was what he was teaching the others—how to give an interesting lecture and not just say "this is a picture of....this is a picture of..." The interns were usually college students who came for the summer to learn. But Jay had others working, as well. School teachers and Indians from the nearby Sioux reservation. Jay would train them for two weeks. Then they went all over the park, taking people on hikes, lecturing in the evenings, and presenting Indian dancers and all sorts of entertainments. Jay's programs were always special and often award winning. Also he edited a book on the park called the "Curious Country" which used some of his photographs. Jay loved the Park Service. It's hard for me to explain just how much.

In WWII Jay joined up because he was about to be drafted. I don't think he went with a bit of patriotic zeal. But he did feel that way about the Park Service. He felt that his work there as a naturalist mattered. He felt the Park Service mattered, that they preserved the wilderness as opposed to the Forest Service which chopped it down. And he didn't object to the Park Service bureaucracy. He didn't mind the regimentation that at times really was like the two of us being back in the first grade. He was just completely in love with that job. He actually felt guilty about taking a salary—which incidentally was the second lowest you could earn as a government employee.

His last year at Badlands, his last year before retirement, he got the second highest award the Department of Interior gave. You had to get the second highest before you got the highest, so he just ran out of time there. Oh, he got awards all the time—and yet none of them really helped. Self-esteem has to come from inside. That's what they say.

I'm certain that I'm reminded of all this because of a dream I had two nights ago. I dreamed we were back in the Badlands National Park. Jay was out walking and I was in the main building doing volunteer work which I often did back then in waking life. Anyway, through the window I saw a helicopter hover and then land. Two men in Park Service uniforms got out, and walking on either side, they escorted Jay into the building—and into the chief naturalist's office.

I started down the hall to see what was happening and there was one of the men coming to get me. They'd already brought in the chief superintendent and the others. And with us all there crowded into the office, they announced that Jay had been appointed Park Service Director. I mean National Director of the entire service. And Jay was so happy. He just beamed. Alive he had never been able to accept the fact that he deserved recognition for all the things he accomplished—for all the beautiful photographs he took, the wilderness he'd worked to preserve, and the people he had helped to educate and assisted in so many ways. Now in the dream he was just radiant. Now, at last, he believed the way he had lived his life meant something. Em says that's God's way of telling me that Jay has found peace. And that dream has made me happy.

Oh, when Jay died I went through the classic torments.

Back then, in every dream Jay was rejecting me. On an emotional level death is that—a rejection. This was a man who on practically every day of our marriage had given me a hug and said, "I love you, Martha." But in the dreams he was divorcing me, he was leaving me. Then gradually in the dreams we began to touch again.

(Doe Hall, S.C. 2001)

JAY

HEART REVISITED

Grief, I did not ask you in.
You came unbidden here to rest.
Now the long task must begin
To exorcise you from my breast.

I must take care lest I accept,
after the first wild tearing pain,
the cloying numbness that has crept
beneath my ribs again.

From: A Confidence on Parting 1967

MARTHA: Death

I was looking out the window last week and there walking across the yard straight towards the house was a turkey vulture. He was walking daintily along, then stopped to pick something up. I went for my binoculars but by then he'd turned away. He'd begun to eat in that same dainty fashion, but I couldn't see what. His meal had a long tail. That I saw. He ate so genteelly. A little bit. A little bit. A little bit. Standing over this unknown animal. When he was almost finished, a second vulture came in and circled. And circled lower. And lower and lower. Until he saw there was not enough left to fight over. He took off. The first vulture kept picking at his meal. He had the most beautiful color to his head. Pinkish red that shown like beautiful polished leather. Finally he flew off. I went outside to investigate. All that was left was the gall bladder. It must have belonged to a big wood rat. But the vulture ate it down to the bitter gall.

On Christmas Eve we'd just started to eat roasted oysters and the phone rang. My nephew Michael said he had found an injured owl on the ground and what to do? I suggested he throw a blanket over it, put it in a box and carry it to the nearby Bird of Prey Center. He did that. The raptor veterinarian thought the owl was young and hadn't learned how to hunt yet. It died that same Christmas night.

The birds: I thought I saw a flock of evening grosbeaks the other day—all yellow and black—fanning colors. I had painted buntings, three pair and at least one pair breeding. They're so rare now a days that a man from the University of Georgia called for information. So many less songbirds around now and so many more grackles and red winged black birds coming to the feeders. I hardly ever see a titmouse, anymore.

I realized I was too dependent on Jay for my happiness. I wanted him to lead me down the path of happiness. After he died I realized how much.. I never would have had the fun I had without Jay in my life. At first I thought he was teasing me about going off to the fire tower in Oregon. Then we went. And kept traveling until his death.

When he died I really didn't know what to do. I spent two summers trying to identify plants. God told me that we all go down to dust. Eventually. But for now I could either cover up my head and die or I could keep looking on my own for that joy that I'd once shared with him. And I have found it. I've found it in nature and with my family and friends.

I've accepted his death. I still don't like the fact. I wish he were back with me.

Lying in bed the other night I saw a meteor shower. I sleep with the shades up for you never know what might go past the window. Once when we were up in the Badlands a group of us were watching the Northern Lights and one of the seasonal naturalists whispered, "CHRREEST!" And one of the Jewish boys whispered, "If that's Christ, what will I do?" Oh, that boy loved Jay and me. They all did. That particular boy went from that internship to eventually become an administrator in the Park Service. When Jay died he wrote me a letter saying he had "basked in the warmth of our love." They all wrote. Practically every intern that Jay had tutored in those Badland days wrote to say something similar.

He'd trained so many of those young Park Service naturalists during his six years at Badlands and earlier at the Carl Sandburg Site, the Blue Ridge and elsewhere. I think I heard from every single one of them—all saying how kind he'd been to them and how much he cared about what they were trying to accomplish.

My husband was a remarkable man.

Oh, we did fight. We did disagree. But not much. Once I told him that if he could learn to eat boiled crabs and read in bed, we'd have a perfect marriage. He said, "I'll come and read in bed with you, but I'll never be able to stand the smell of boiled crabs." Actually, he didn't eat much seafood or game. That's all his daddy had fed them during the Depression. But I liked seafood and game for exactly the same reason. So our taste weren't identical.

When I was nine, my friend Amy asked me who I was going to marry, I answered "Bunny." That's what we called Jay. I wasn't really thinking about marriage, but even at nine he was my best friend. He was so sensitive, too sensitive. When he ran through that field and stepped on the baby rabbit, he sat down and sobbed. And I thought this is the person I want to spend my life with.

Our family doctor called me into his office and said he was concerned with Jay's memory lapses. I didn't want to hear that. I just denied all that. Eventually, I had to face up to the facts. Jay went off to take trash to the dump and returned without his precious dog. I asked, "Where's Wolfie?" He said, "Wolfie didn't go with me." Wolfie stayed lost for one desperate night. Then Jay had a little wreck at the post office, a bent fender. The change seemed gradual but looking back, I suppose it was rapid. One morning I went off to the post office and returned to find he'd accidentally locked me out. And he couldn't figure out how to unlock the door. Finally I got him over to the elevator. I called up, "You see the "down" button?" He pushed the button and I was able to ride up in the elevator.

Then he started wandering at night. He couldn't sleep. I'd find him trying to hide or going through a box on the floor—sifting through the Styrofoam packaging. I'd be lucky to get three hours of sleep. I had new locks on the door, but I was still afraid he'd somehow unlock them and go outside. I couldn't close my eyes. Then Jay started getting mad with me, striking out at me, and I knew something had to be done. With the help of our doctor, I got him into a neurological clinic at Charleston's Medical University. Once there, a specialist ordered a brain biopsy. He suspected a growth on the thalamus which is what he found. He diagnosed Jay as having Lewy body dementia. The signs are the same as for Alzheimer's but the deterioration is much faster and the weight loss is more dramatic. Jay went from 220 pounds to less than 100.

Perhaps Jay had Alzheimer's as well. When he went into the nursing home they called it Alzheimer's. Jay gave his body to the Medical University, and I didn't ask for an autopsy. I didn't know it was necessary to ask.

The doctor at the Medical University wrote me a wonderful letter saying how happy he was to have known Jay before he went completely...I'm certain the doctor was right in his diagnosis and thankful in the sense that I was spared ten years of nursing homes.

After just one week of visiting Jay in the hospital, I told our own doctor I couldn't go on. He understood and arranged for Jay to go from there into a nursing home. Before entering the hospital, I had been walking with Jay in our yard and asked him if he knew where he was. He said, "No." We walked further away from the house and looked back. I said, "Whose house is that?" He said, "I don't know!" And then he hit me. That was so unlike my husband. He would have been horrified to know he had hit me. But I knew that wasn't my Jay.

In the nursing home, Jay would whisper for me to get down on the floor. He'd say, "Quick. They're going to shoot us." Then he'd yell out. Jay had been with me always. I had to put his mattress down on the floor. He'd started to crawl out—to fall out of bed. In those last days, I would lie on the mattress beside him and hold him in my arms.

Jay had been a part of my life for all of my life. And I still miss him.

(Doe Hall, S.C. 2001)

Chapter Four

“Mart, look at this……..”

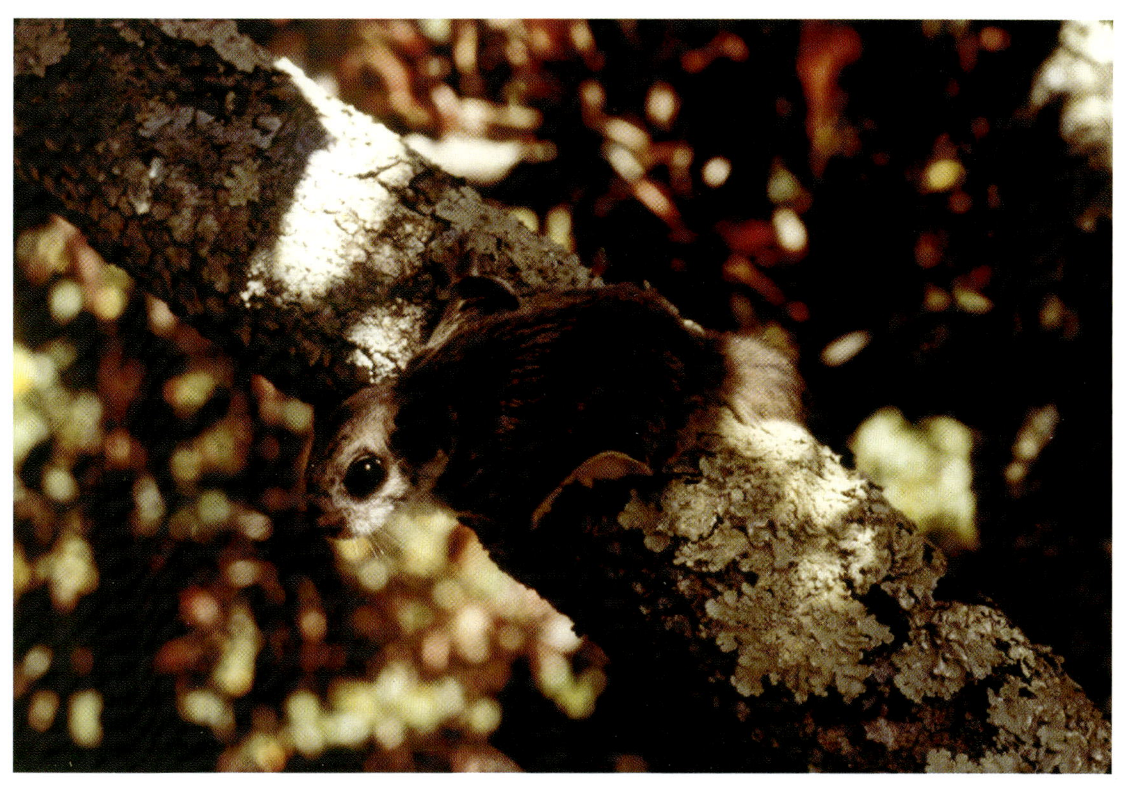

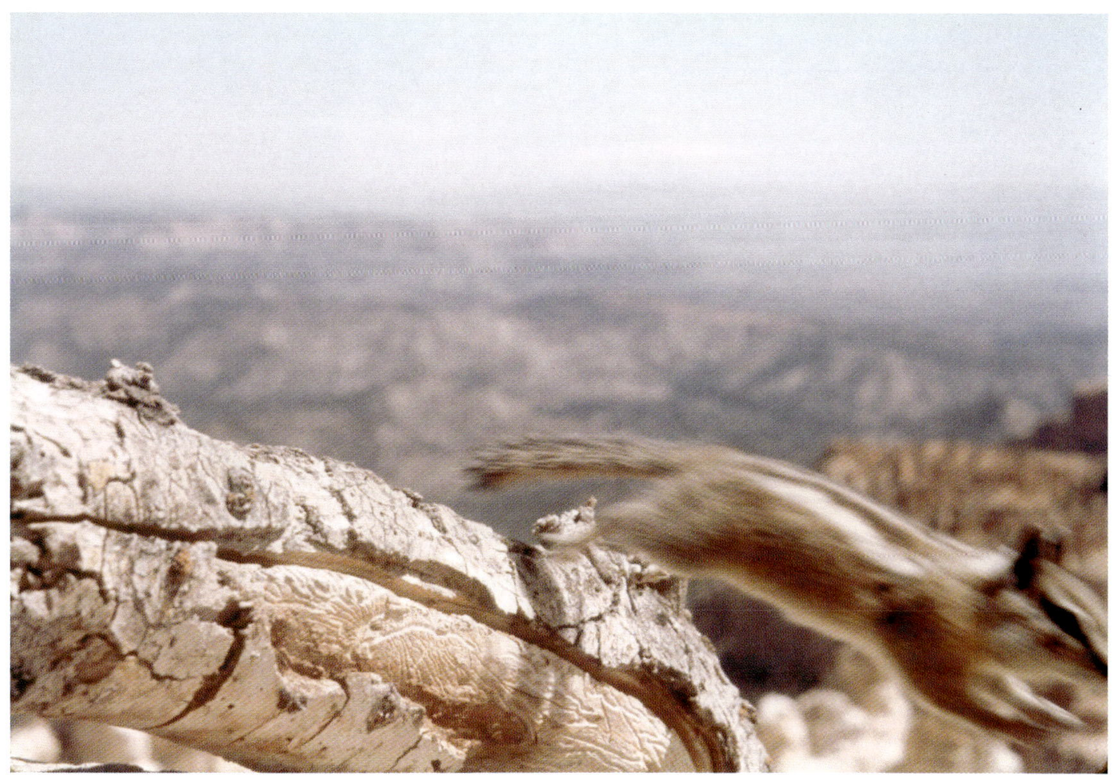

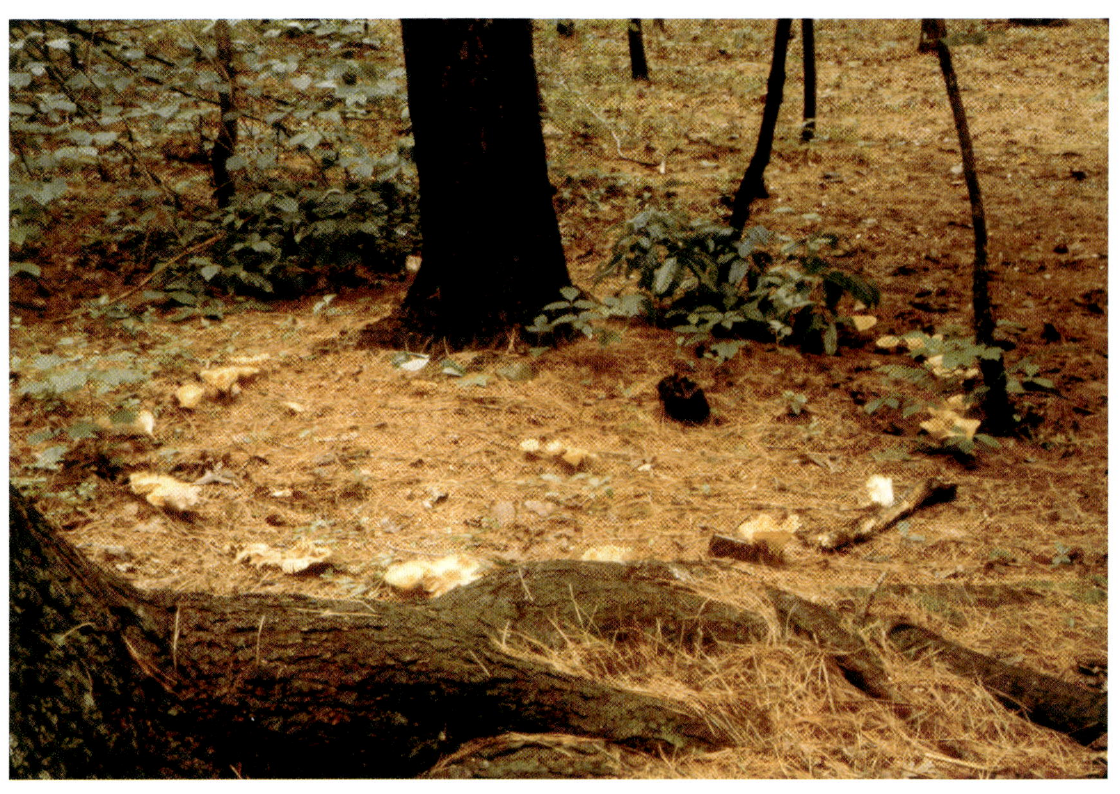

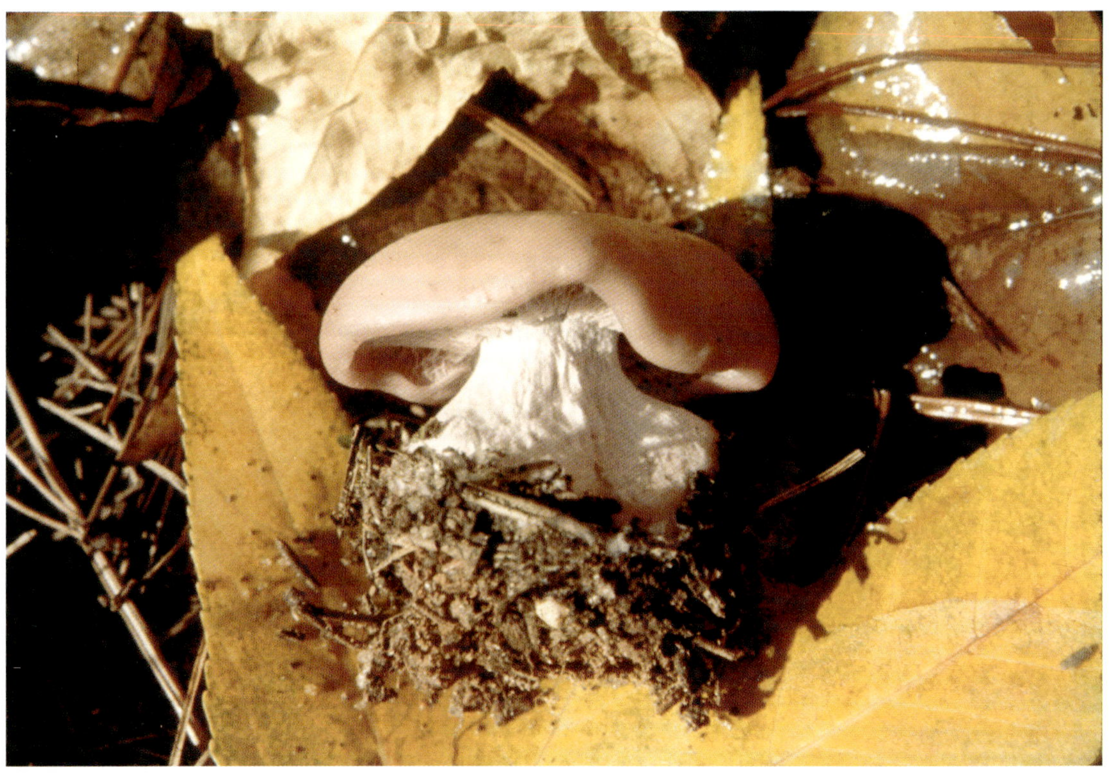

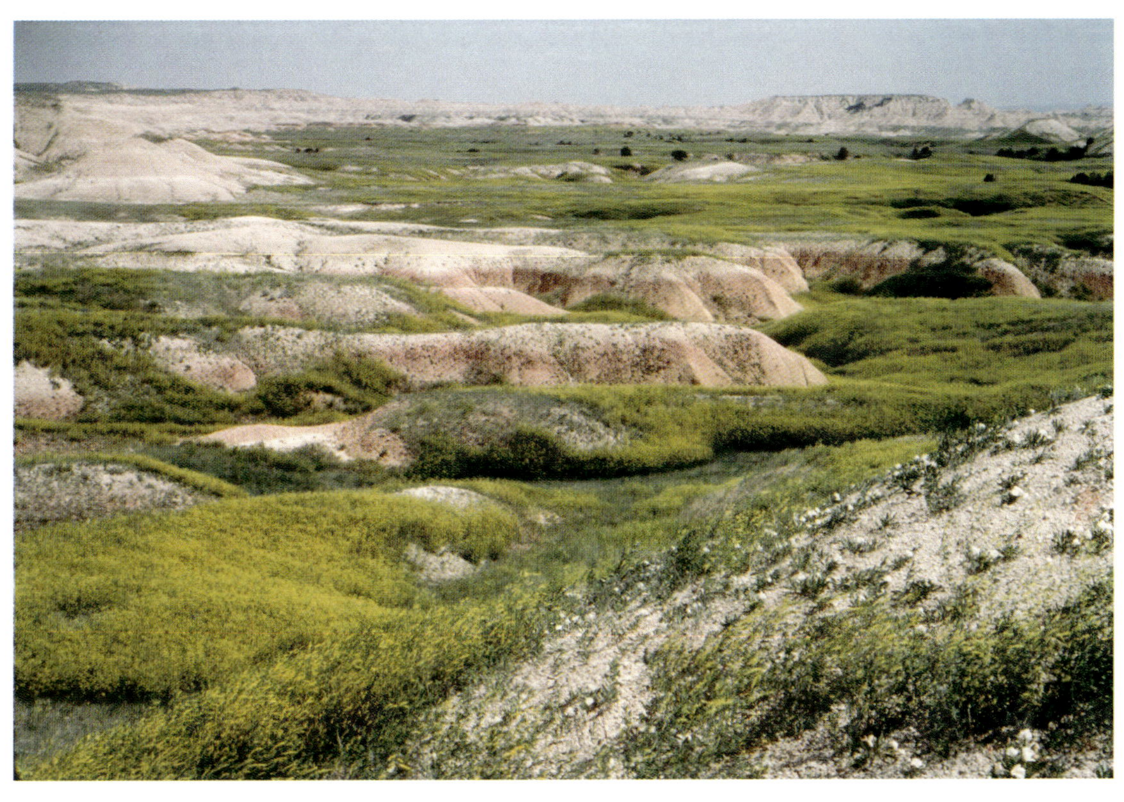

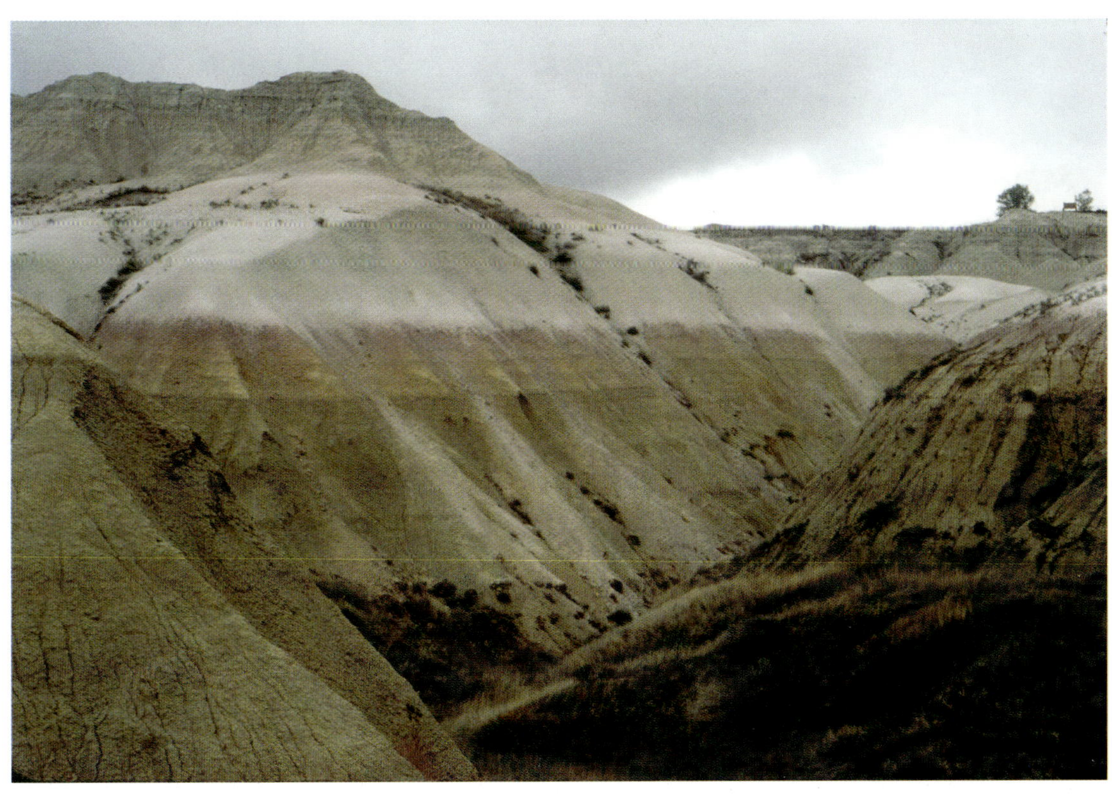

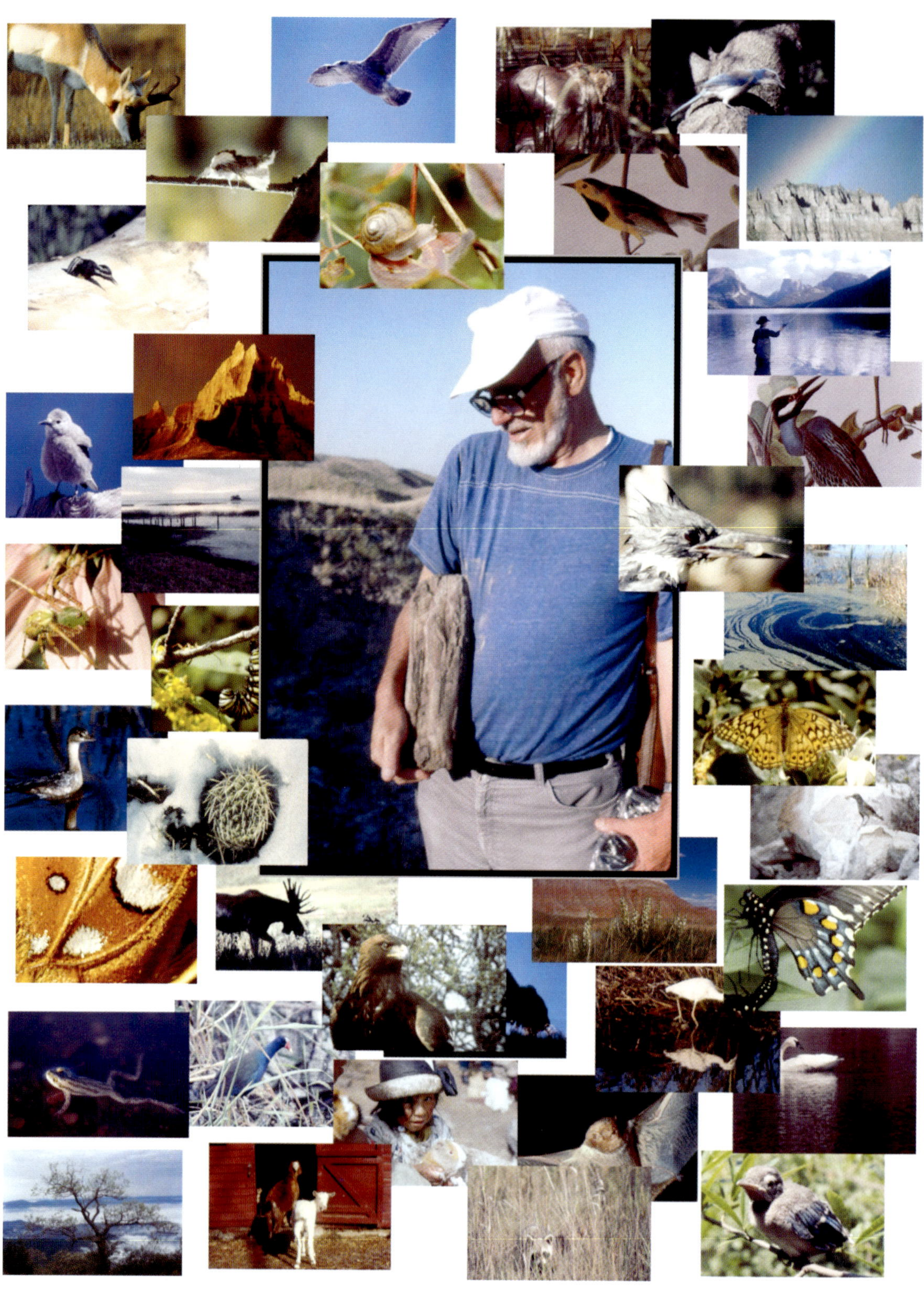

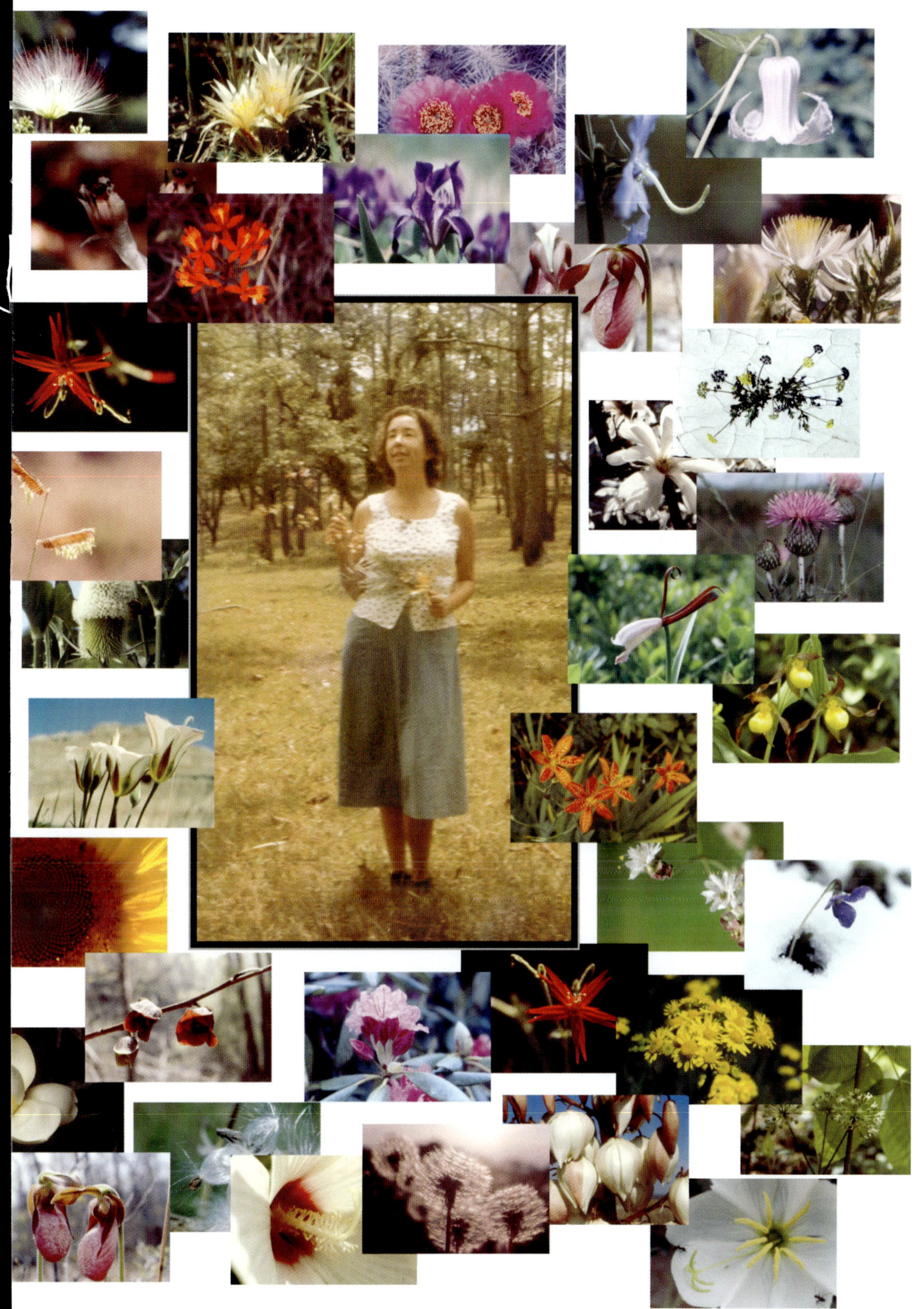

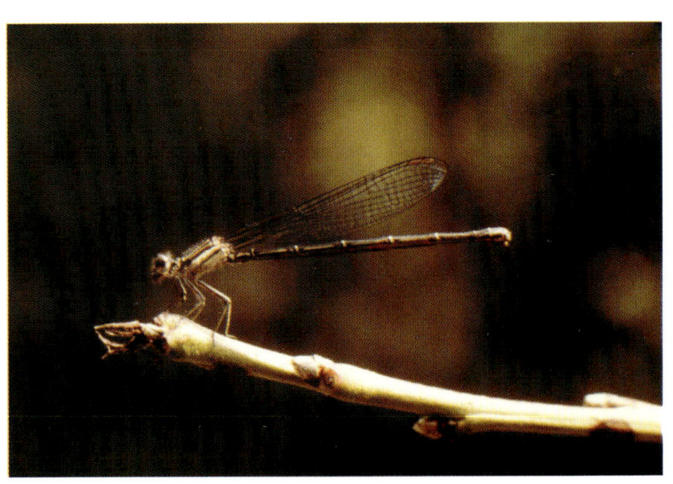

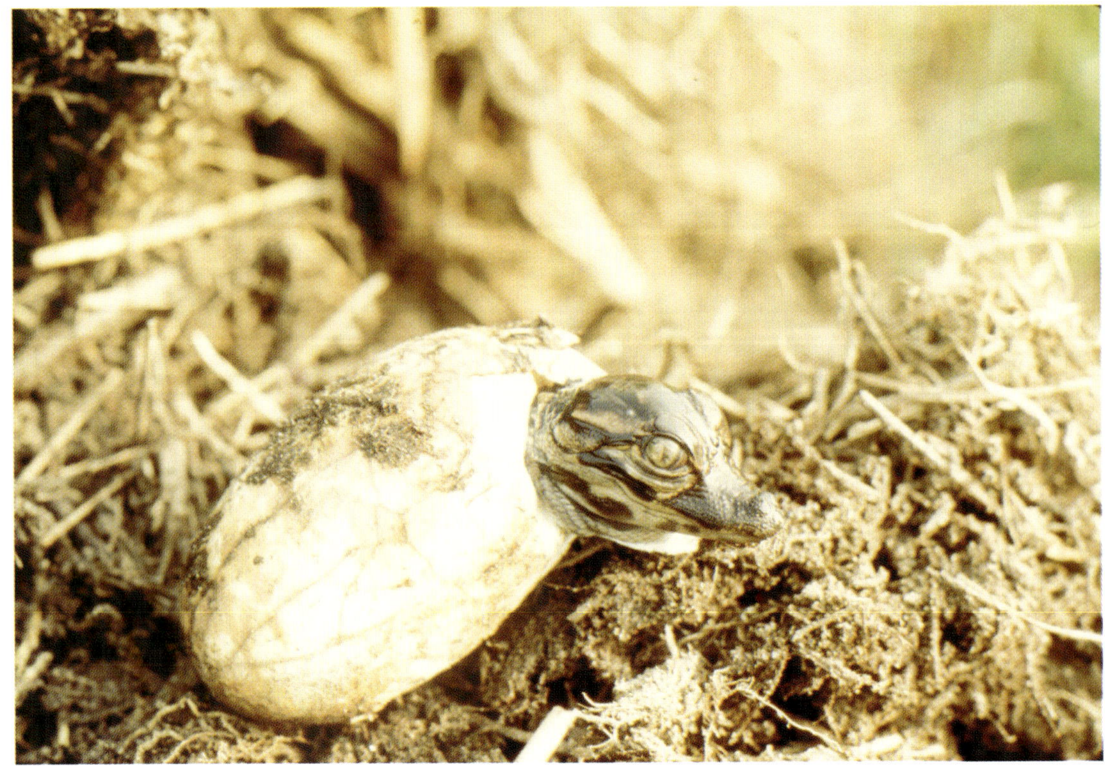

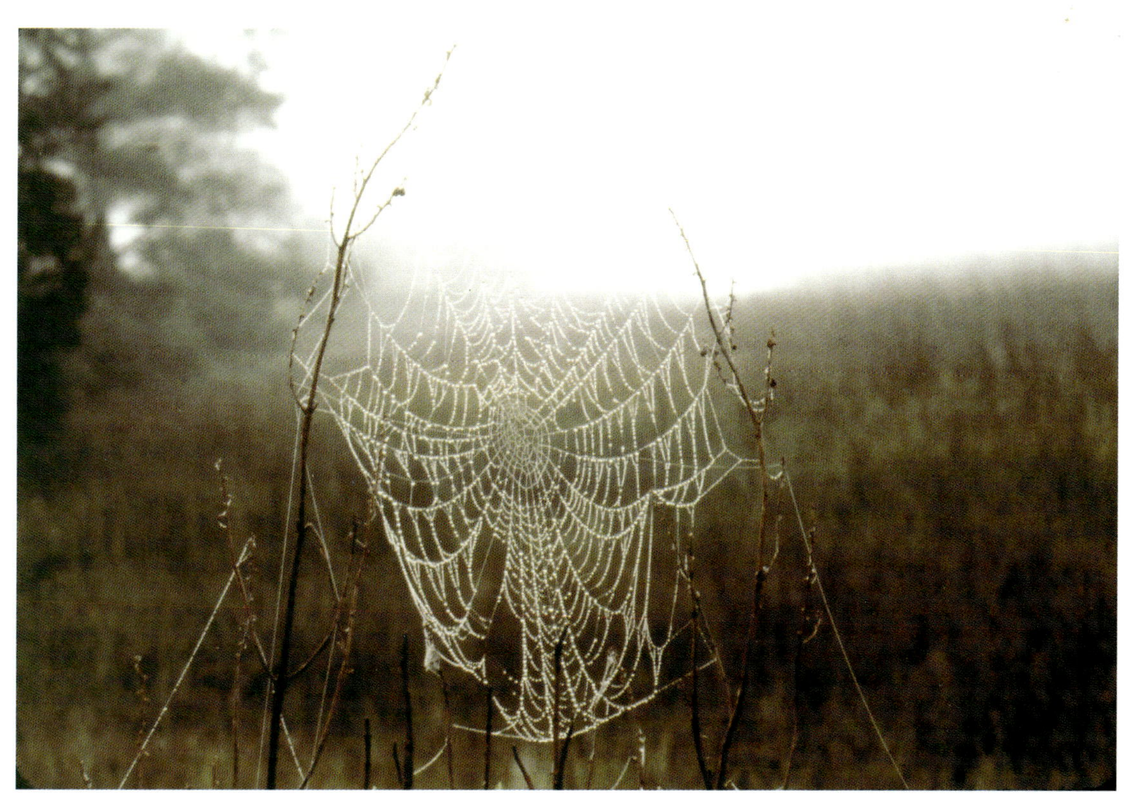

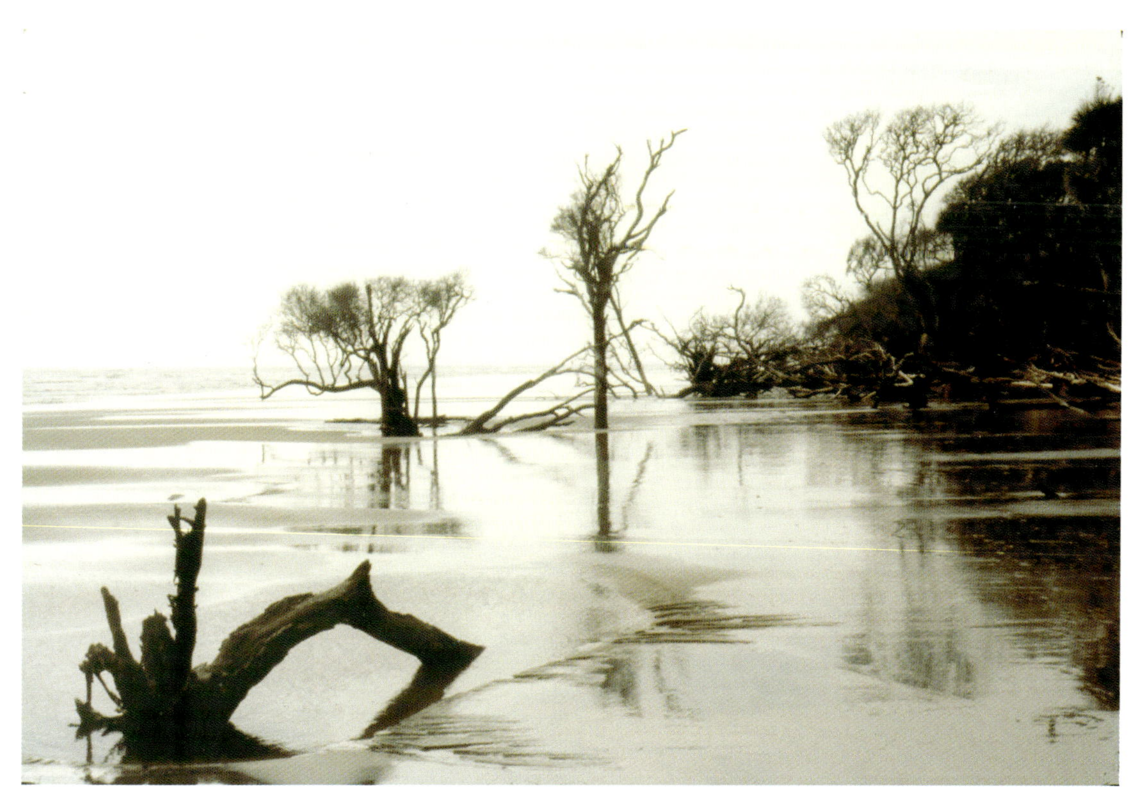

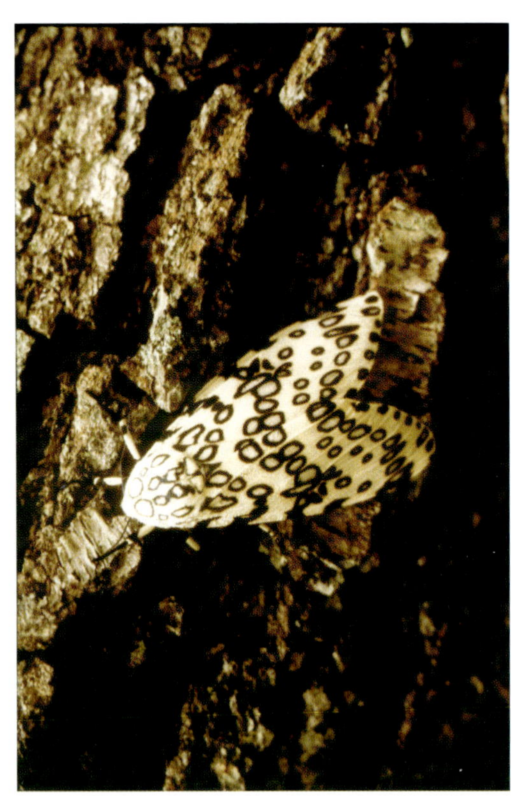

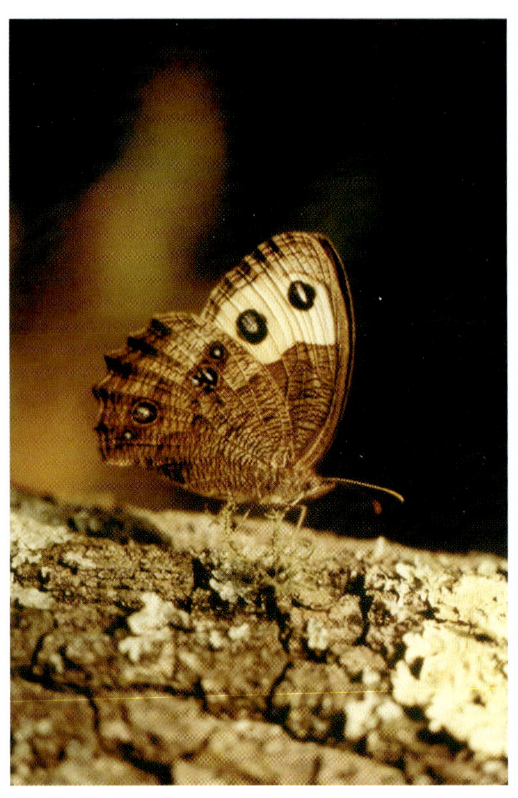

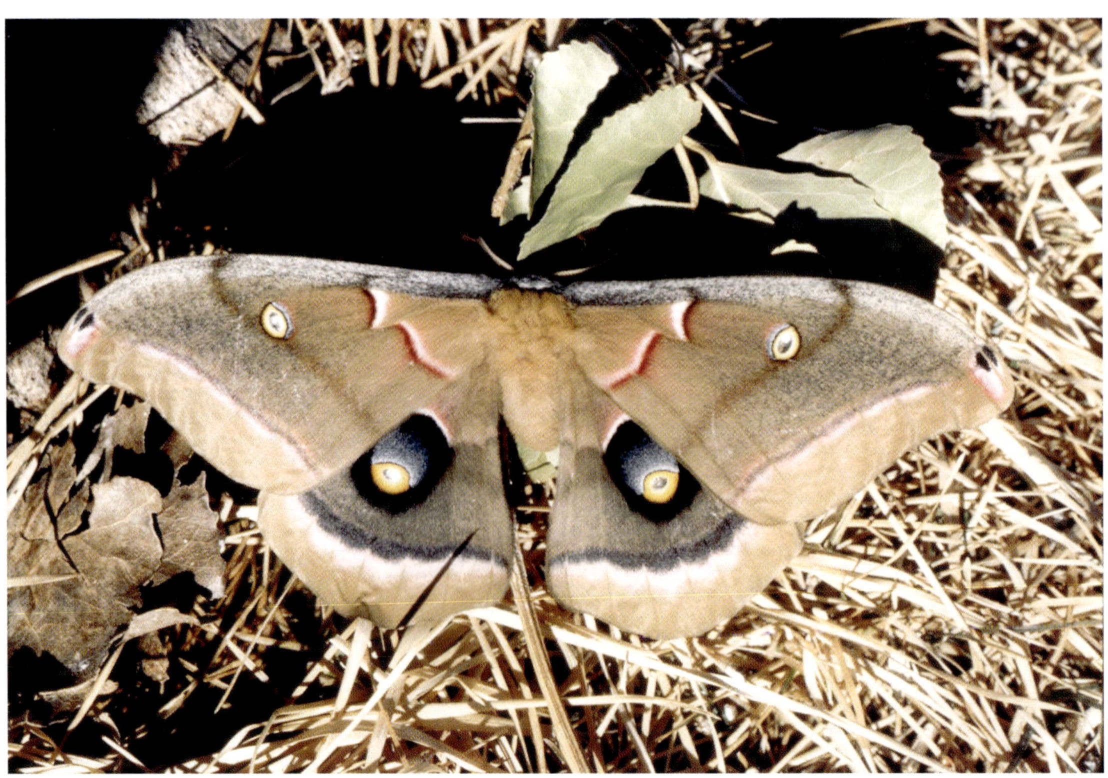

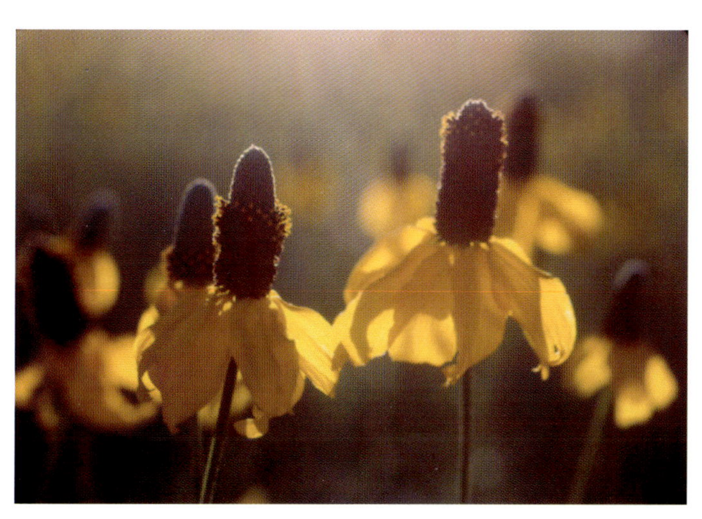

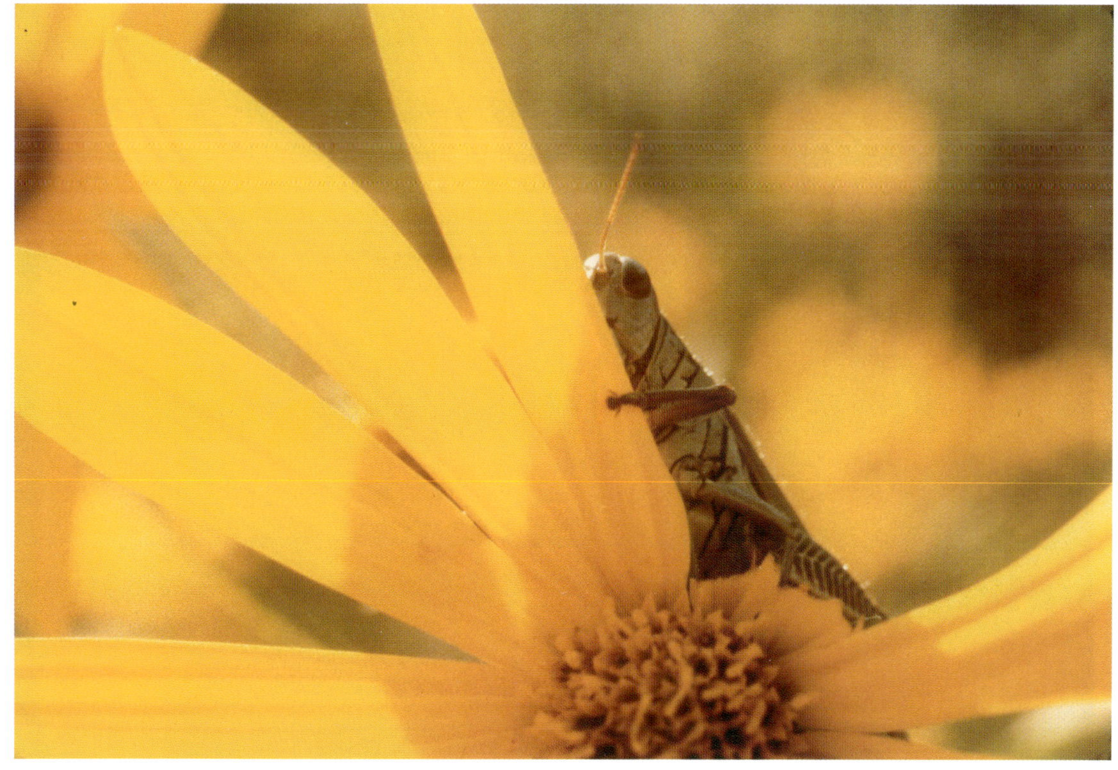

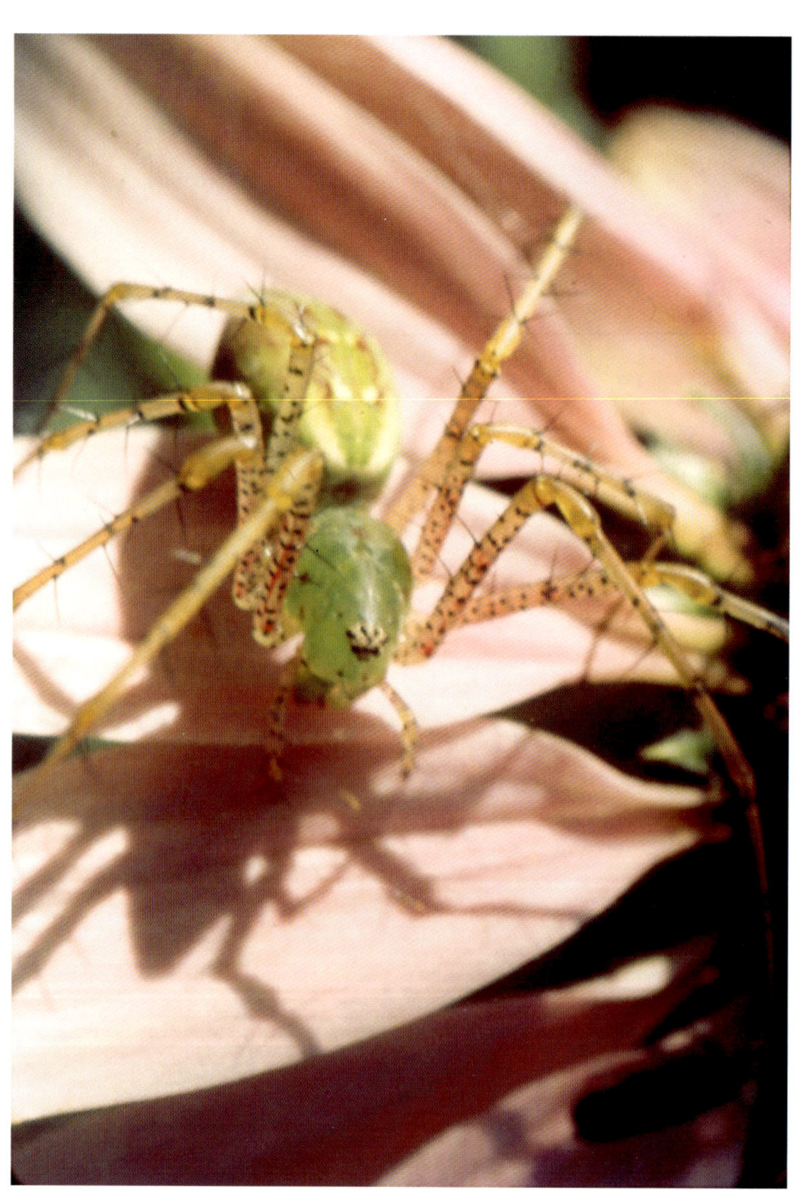

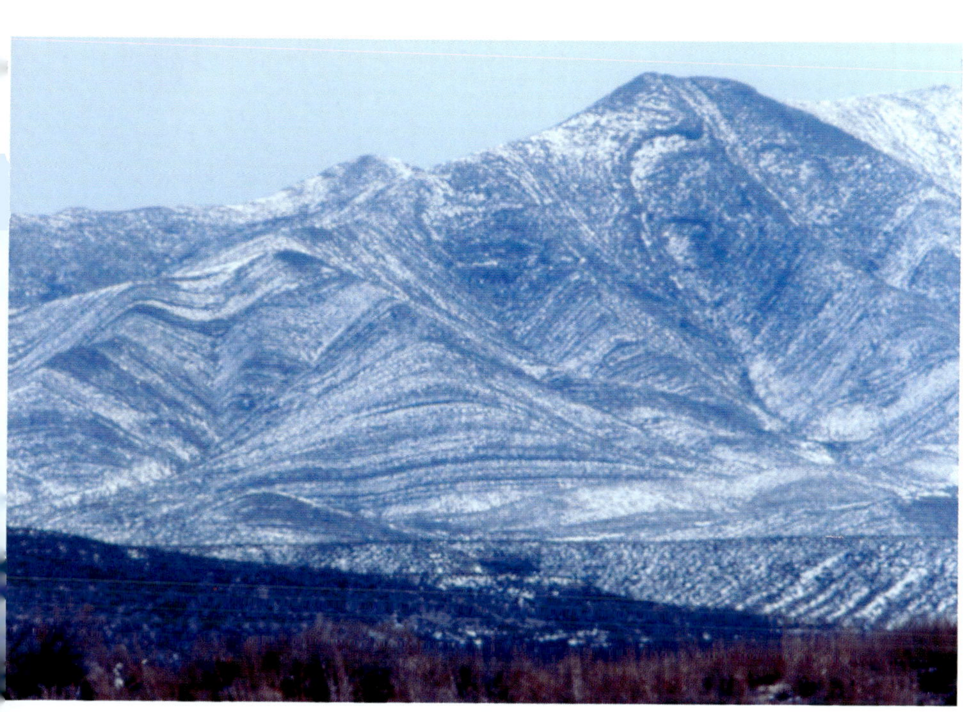

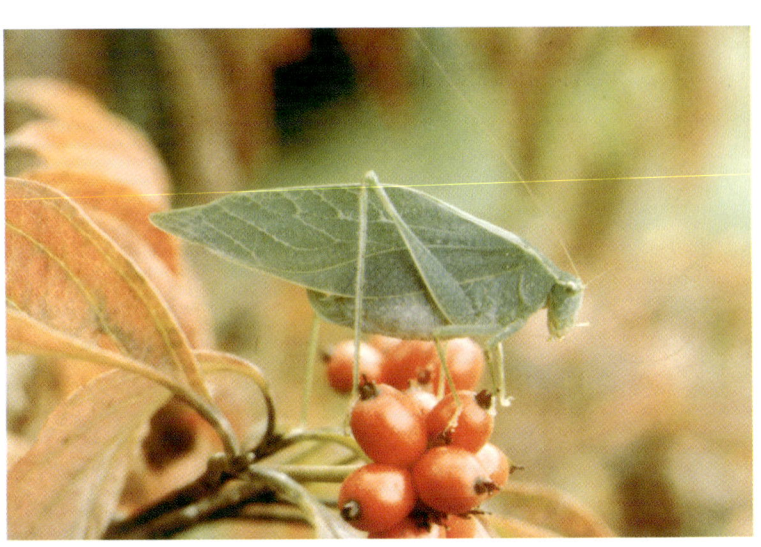